Adventures in Yellowstone

Early Travelers Tell Their Tales

M. Mark Miller

TWODOT®

GUILFORD, CONNECTICUT
HELENA, MONTANA
AN IMPRINT OF THE GLOBE PEQUOT PRESS

T W O D O T

Copyright © 2009 by M. Mark Miller

TwoDot is a registered trademark of Morris Book Publishing, LLC.

Project editor: Julie Marsh
Text design: Sheryl P. Kober
Layout: Joanna Beyer
Map © Robert Kyllo/Shutterstock

Adventures in Yellowstone : early travelers tell their tales / [compiled by] M. Mark Miller.
    p. cm.
  Includes bibliographical references.
  ISBN 978-0-7627-5414-4
  1. Yellowstone National Park—Description and travel—Sources. 2. Yellowstone National Park—History—Sources. I. Miller, M. Mark.
  F722.A34 2009
  917.87'52042—dc22
                     2009013812

Printed in the United States of America
10 9 8 7 6 5 4 3 2 1

Dedicated to the memory of my grandmother Theora Mercer Nolte, who told me marvelous stories about her trip to Yellowstone National Park in 1909 and her uncle, father, grandfather's trip there in 1882.

Contents

Preface

When I was a little boy, my grandmother told me marvelous stories about going to Yellowstone Park. She went there in 1909 with her aunt, seven cousins, and two brothers. They had a covered wagon for food and camping equipment, a surrey for the aunt and small children, and five saddle horses. The trip took four weeks and they camped out every night.

Grandma rode astride at a time when ladies were supposed to use sidesaddles. She recalled seeing geysers, catching fish, and baking bread in hot springs. She also told stories about her father, grandfather, and uncle who went to Yellowstone in 1880. One of their favorite tricks, she said, was stealing one another's red flannel underwear and tossing it into a geyser to tint the next eruption pink.

I loved Grandma's stories and decided to see if I could find more like them. People always knew their trips to Yellowstone were special so they left diaries, reminiscences, newspaper and magazine articles, and books about them. I have read more than two hundred first-person accounts of travel to Yellowstone. I found most of them in collections at the Pioneer Museum of Bozeman, the Montana State University Libraries, and the Yellowstone Park Research Center in Gardiner, Montana. Some come from other sources such as family papers and the Internet.

Many accounts are little more than mundane descriptions of the weather and the sights. But others tell of such exciting events as being mauled by bears, scalded in geysers, or captured by Indians. I have collected the best of those stories here.

I am a storyteller, not a historian. I chose accounts that were well told and that described interesting experiences. I didn't fret over their literal truth. No doubt many of these stories contain exaggerations and embellishments, perhaps even outright fabrications. Throughout this process, my focus has been on putting together an anthology of some of the most vivid and gripping historical stories related to Yellowstone—and to present these pieces in a manner compelling to modern readers. Many of these pieces were written in an archaic style or contain obscure references and grammatical errors. In some cases, I've taken the liberty of editing for readability. A few of the longer pieces such as full-length books have been abridged to focus on dramatic stories and events. In the interest of creating a more enjoyable reading experience, I've most often forgone certain editorial conventions, such as ellipses to indicate omissions, and I've updated archaic spellings.

Many people helped in the preparation of this book. I am grateful to Humanities Montana, which provided motivation by including me in their impressive Speakers Bureau. Too many people to name assisted me, but I particularly want to thank Ann Butterfield of the Pioneer Museum and Kim Allen Scott of the Montana State University Libraries. Also, thanks to the volunteers of the Pioneer Museum who paid polite attention to various drafts and provided bounteous encouragement. These people made the book better, but, of course, I take responsibility for any errors.

Finally, I want to thank my wife, Tam, for financial and moral support.

OSBORNE RUSSELL

—m—

The first white man to see the wonders of what is now Yellowstone National Park was John Colter, a member of the Lewis and Clark Expedition. On the expedition's return trip in 1806, Colter got permission to leave the group and set off on his own with a pair of trappers. While looking for Indians to trade with, Colter passed through Yellowstone in 1807.

Mountain men like Joe Meek and Jim Bridger went throughout the Rockies trading and trapping until 1840, when the bottom fell out of the fur market. After that, most mountain men disappeared, leaving few marks on the land. Their tales about Yellowstone's wonders were greeted with skepticism. It's no surprise that people didn't believe their stories about waterfalls that fell a thousand feet or fountains of boiling water hundreds of feet tall. They were mostly illiterates who dressed in animal skins and took Indian women as wives. Besides, they often entertained themselves by seeing who could tell the biggest whopper.

Osborne Russell was one of few who left a credible written record. Russell, who worked for several trapping and trading companies, joined Jim Bridger's brigade of the Rocky Mountain Fur Company when it went through Yellowstone in 1839.

Russell left his mark on history through the detailed and brightly written account he wrote from notes in the 1840s. It is one of very few contemporary accounts of the daily lives

of mountain men. He tells about the food they ate, the shel-
ters they used, and how they traveled. Here are some excerpts
beginning when Russell was traveling near Shoshone Lake
on the southwest side of what is now Yellowstone National
Park. The geyser he describes is apparently now defunct.

GEYSERS AND BLACKFEET—1839

Excerpted from Osborne Russell's
Journal of a Trapper

We traveled along the border of the lake till we came to the northwest extremity where we found about fifty springs of boiling hot water. We stopped here some hours because one of my comrades had visited this spot the year previous and he wished to show us some curiosities.

The first spring we visited was about ten feet in diameter and threw up mud with a noise similar to boiling soap. Close about this were numerous similar to it throwing up hot mud and water five or six feet high. About thirty or forty paces from these, along the side of a small ridge, the hot steam rushed forth from holes in the ground, with a hissing noise that could be heard a mile distant.

After surveying these natural wonders for some time, my comrade conducted me to what he called the "Hour Spring." At this spring the first thing that attracted attention was a hole about fifteen inches in diameter in which the water was boiling slowly about four inches below the surface. At length it began to boil and bubble violently, and the water commenced raising and shooting upwards until the column arose to the height of sixty feet, from whence it fell to the ground in drops in a circle of about thirty feet in diameter, perfectly cold when it struck the ground.

It continued shooting up in this manner five or six minutes and then sank back to its former state of slowly boiling for an hour—and then it would shoot forth again as before. My comrade said he had watched the motions of this spring for one whole day and part of the night the year previous and found no irregularity whatever in its movements.

After surveying these wonders for a few hours we left the place and traveled north about three miles over ascending ground, then descended a steep and rugged mountain four miles in the same direction and fell onto the head branch of the Jefferson branch of the Missouri. The whole country was still thickly covered with pines except here and there a small prairie. We encamped and set some traps for beaver and stayed four days.

At this place there was also a large number of hot springs, some of which had formed cones of limestone twenty feet high of a snowy whiteness, which makes a splendid appearance standing among the evergreen pines. Some of the lower peaks are very convenient for the hunter in preparing his dinner when hungry, for here his kettle is always ready and boiling. His meat being suspended in the water on a string is soon prepared for his meal without further trouble.

We encamped on the Yellowstone in the big plain below the lake. The next day we went to the lake and set our traps on a branch running into it, near the outlet on the northeast side.

After visiting my traps, I returned to the camp, where, after stopping for about an hour or two, I took my rifle and sauntered down the shore of the lake among the scattered groves of tall pines until tired of walking about (the day being very warm), I took a bath in the lake, probably half an hour, and returned to the camp about four o'clock.

Two of my comrades observed: "Let us take a walk among the pines and kill an elk," and started off, while the other was still asleep. Sometime after they were gone I went to a bale of dried meat, which had been spread in the sun thirty or forty feet from the place where we slept. Here I pulled off my powder horn and bullet pouch and laid them on a log—drew my butcher knife and began to cut.

After eating a few minutes, I arose and kindled a fire, filled my tobacco pipe and sat down to smoke. My comrade, whose name was White, was still sleeping. Presently, I cast my eyes towards the horses, which were feeding in the valley and discovered the heads of some Indians gliding round within thirty steps of me.

I jumped to my rifle and aroused White. Looking towards my powder horn and bullet pouch, I saw they were already in the hands of an Indian, and we were completely surrounded. We cocked our rifles and started through their ranks into the woods, which seemed to be completely filled with Blackfeet, who rent the air with their horrid yells.

On presenting our rifles they opened a space about twenty feet wide, through which we plunged. About the fourth jump, an arrow struck White on the right hip joint. I hastily told him to pull it out and as I spoke another arrow struck me in the same place, but the arrows did not retard our progress. Another arrow struck through my right leg above the knee and I fell with my breast across a log. The Indian who shot me was within eight feet of me and made a spring towards me with his uplifted battle ax. I made a leap and avoided the blow and kept hopping from log to log through a shower of arrows that flew around us like hail, lodging in the pines and logs.

After we had passed them about ten paces we wheeled about and took aim at them. They began to dodge behind the trees and shoot their guns. We then ran and hopped about fifty yards farther in the logs and bushes and made a stand.

I was very faint from the loss of blood, and we sat down among the logs, determined to kill the two foremost when they came up and then die like men. We rested our rifles across a log—White aiming at the foremost and myself at the second. I whispered to him that when they turned their eyes towards us to pull trigger.

About twenty of them passed by us within fifteen feet without casting a glance towards us. Another file came round on the opposite side within twenty or thirty paces, closing with the first a few rods beyond us and all turning to the right. The next minute they were out of our sight among the bushes. They were all well armed with fusees, bows, and battle axes.

We sat until the rustling among the bushes had died away, then arose, and after looking carefully around us, White asked in a whisper how far it was to the lake. I replied, pointing to the southeast, about a quarter of a mile. I was nearly fainting from the loss of blood and the want of water.

We hobbled along forty or fifty rods and I was obliged to sit down for a few minutes, then go a little further, and then rest again. We managed in this way until we reached the bank of the lake. Our next object was to obtain some of the water as the bank was very steep and high. White had been perfectly calm and deliberate, but now his conversation became wild, hurried, and despairing. He observed, "I cannot go down to that water for I am wounded all over. I shall die." I told him to sit down while I crawled down and brought some in my hat. This I effected with a great deal of difficulty.

We then hobbled along the border of the lake for a mile and a half, until it grew dark and we stopped. We could still hear the shouting of the savages over their booty. We stopped under a large pine near the lake, and I told White I could go no further.

"Oh," said he, "let us go up into the pines and find a spring."

I replied there was no spring within a mile of us, which I knew to be a fact.

"Well," said he, "if you stop here I shall make a fire."

"Make as much as you please," I replied angrily. "This is a poor time now to undertake to frighten me into measures."

I then started to the spring, crawling on my hands and one knee, and returned in about an hour with some water in my hat.

While I was at this he had kindled a small fire and, taking a draught of water from the hat, he exclaimed, "Oh, dear, we shall die here; we shall never get out of these mountains."

"Well," said I, "if you persist in thinking so, you will die, but I can crawl from this place upon my hands and one knee and kill two or three elk and make a shelter of the skins, and dry the meat, until we get able to travel."

In this manner I persuaded him that we were not in half so bad a situation as we might be, although he was not in half so bad a situation as I expected, for, on examining him I found only a slight wound from an arrow on his hip bone. But he was not so much to blame, as he was a young man who had been brought up in Missouri, the pet of the family, and had never done or learned much of anything but horse racing and gambling while under the care of his parents (if care it could be called).

I pulled off an old piece of a coat made of blanket (as he was entirely without clothing except his hat and shirt), set myself in a leaning position against a tree, ever and anon gathering such leaves and rubbish as I could reach without altering the position of my body, to keep up a little fire, and in this manner miserably spent the night.

The next morning I could not arise without assistance, when White procured a couple of sticks for crutches, by the help of which I hobbled to a small grove of pines about sixty yards distant. We had scarcely entered the grove when we heard a dog barking and Indians singing and talking. The sound seemed to be approaching us. They at length came near to where we were, to the number of sixty.

They commenced shooting at a large bank of elk that was swimming in the lake, killed four of them, dragged them to shore and butchered them, which occupied about three hours. They then packed the meat in small bundles on their backs and traveled up along the rocky shore about a mile and encamped.

We then left our hiding place and crept into the thick pines about fifty yards distant and started in the direction of our encampment in the hope of finding our comrades. My leg was very much swollen and painful, but I managed to get along slowly on my crutches with White carrying my rifle.

When we were within about sixty rods of the encampment we discovered the Canadian, hunting round among the trees as though he was looking for a trail. We approached him within thirty feet before he saw us, and he was so much agitated by fear that he knew not whether to run or stand still.

On being asked where Elbridge was, he said they came to the camp the night before at sunset. The Indians pursued them into the woods, where they separated, and he saw him no more.

At the encampment I found a sack of salt. Everything else the Indians had carried away or cut to pieces. They had built seven large conical forts near the spot, from which we supposed their number to have been seventy or eighty, part of whom had returned to their Village with the horses and plunder. We left the place, heaping curses on the head of the Blackfeet nation, which neither injured them nor alleviated our distress.

We followed down the shores of the lake and stopped for the night. My companions threw some logs and rubbish together, forming a kind of shelter from the night breeze. But in the night it took fire (the logs being of pitch pine) and the blaze ran to the tops of the trees.

We removed a short distance, built another fire and laid by it until morning. We then made a raft of dry poles and crossed the outlet upon it. We then went to a small grove of pines nearby and made a fire, where we stopped the remainder of the day in hopes that Elbridge would see our signals and come to us, for we left directions on a tree at the encampment which route we would take. In the meantime, the Canadian went to hunt something to eat but without success. I had bathed my wounds in saltwater and made a salve of beaver's oil and castoreum, which I applied to them. This had eased the pain and drawn out the swelling in a great measure.

The next morning I felt very stiff and sore, but we were obliged to travel or starve, as we had eaten nothing since our defeat and game was very scarce on the west side of the lake. Moreover, the Canadian had got such a fright we could not prevail on him to go out of our sight to hunt.

So on we trudged slowly, and after getting warm I could bear half my weight on my lame leg, although it was bent considerably and swelled so much that my knee joint was stiff. About ten o'clock the Canadian killed a couple of small ducks, which served us for breakfast. After eating them we pursued our journey.

At twelve o'clock it began to rain, but we still kept on until the sun was two hours high in the evening, when the weather cleared away. We encamped at some hot springs and killed a couple of geese.

While we were eating them, a deer came swimming along in the lake within about one hundred yards of the shore. We fired several shots at him, but with the water glancing the balls, he remained unhurt and apparently unalarmed. He still kept swimming to and fro in the lake in front of us for an hour and then started along up close to the shore.

The hunter went to watch it in order to kill it when it should come ashore. But as he was lying in wait for the deer, a doe elk came to the water to drink, and he killed her, the deer being still out in the lake swimming to and fro till dark.

Now we had a plenty of meat and drink but were almost destitute of clothing. I had on a pair of trousers and a cotton shirt, which were completely drenched with the rain. We made a sort of shelter from the wind of pine branches and built a large fire of pitch knots in front of it, so that we were burning on one side and freezing on the other, alternately, all night.

The next morning we cut some of the elk meat in thin slices and cooked it slowly over a fire, then packed it in bundles, strung them on our backs and started. By this time I could carry my own rifle and limp along half as fast as a man could walk, but when my foot touched against the logs or brush, the pain in my leg was very severe.

We left the lake at the hot springs and traveled through the thick pines, over a low ridge of land, through the snow and rain. We came to a lake about twelve miles in circumference, which is the headspring of the right branch of Lewis Fork. Here we found a dry spot near a number of hot springs under some thick pines. Our hunter had killed a deer on the way, and I took the skin, wrapped it around me and felt prouder of my mantle than a monarch with his imperial robes.

This night I slept more than four hours, which was more than I had slept at any one time since I was wounded, and arose the next morning much refreshed.

These springs are similar to those on the Madison, and among these, as well as those, sulphur is found in its purity in large quantities on the surface of the ground. We traveled along the shore on the south side about five miles in an east direction, fell in with a large band of elk, killed two fat does and took some of the meat. We then left the lake and traveled due south over a rough, broken country, covered with thick pines, for about twelve miles, when we came to the fork again, which ran through a narrow prairie bottom, followed down it about six miles and encamped at the forks. We had passed up the lefthand fork on horseback, in good health and spirits, and came down on the right bank on foot, with weary limbs and sorrowful countenances. We built a fire and laid down to rest, but I could not sleep more than fifteen or twenty minutes at a time, the night being so very cold. We had plenty of meat, however, and made moccasins of raw elk hide. The next day we crossed the stream and traveled down near to Jackson's Lake on the west side, then took up a small branch in a west direction to the head. We then had the Teton Mountain to cross, which looked like a laborious undertaking as it was steep and the top covered with snow. We arrived at the summit however with a great deal of difficulty, before sunset, and after resting a few moments traveled down about a mile on the other side and stopped for the night.

After spending another cold and tedious night, we were descending the mountain through the pines at daylight and the next night reached the forks of Henry's Fork of Snake River. This day was very warm, but the wind blew cold at night. We made a fire and gathered some dry grass to sleep on and then sat down and ate the remainder of our provisions.

It was now ninety miles to Fort Hall, and we expected to see little or no game on the route, but we determined to travel it in three days. We lay down and shivered with the cold till daylight, then arose and again pursued our journey towards the fork of Snake River, where we arrived with the sun about an hour high, forded the river, which was nearly swimming, and encamped. The weather being very cold and fording the river so late at night caused me much suffering during the night.

September 4th we were on our way at daybreak and traveled all day through the high sage and sand down Snake River. We stopped at dark, nearly worn out with fatigue, hunger and want of sleep, as we had now traveled sixty-five miles in two days without eating. We sat and hovered over a small fire until another day appeared, then set out as usual and traveled to within about ten miles of the Fort when I was seized with a cramp in my wounded leg, which compelled me to stop and sit down every thirty or forty rods. At length we discovered a half-breed encamped in the valley, who furnished us with horses and went with us to the fort, where we arrived naked, hungry, wounded, sleepy, and fatigued, with the sun being about an hour high. Here again I entered a trading post after being defeated by the Indians, but the treatment was quite different from that which I had received at Savonery's Fork in 1837, when I had been defeated by the Crows.

The fort was in the charge of Mr. Courtney M. Walker, who had been lately employed by the Hudson Bay Company for that purpose. He invited us into a room and ordered supper to be prepared immediately—likewise such articles of clothing and blankets as we called for.

After dressing ourselves and giving a brief history of our defeat and sufferings, supper was brought in, consisting of tea, cakes, buttermilk, dried meat, etc. I ate very sparingly as I had been three days fasting, but drank so much strong tea that it kept me awake till after midnight.

I continued to bathe my leg in warm saltwater and applied a salve, which healed it in a very short time, so that in ten days I was again setting traps for beaver.

NATHANIEL PITT LANGFORD

—⧟—

After the collapse of the beaver trapping industry in the 1840s, the upper Yellowstone was neglected for nearly two decades. Then the discovery of gold in the 1860s brought thousands of treasure hunters into the Northern Rockies. Those who prospected the upper Yellowstone brought back reports of strange and wonderful things. At first people discounted the reports as tall tales in the tradition of the mountain men, but the stories were so consistent that it became obvious that there really was something there.

Soon there was talk of an exploring party to find out once and for all what existed in the upper Yellowstone. Several expedition plans fell through because organizers couldn't raise big enough parties to ward off Indian attacks. Finally the rumors sparked interest among several other men who organized what became the Washburn Expedition of 1870.

Several members of the Washburn Expedition were public officials and prominent businessmen whose credibility could not be doubted. Also, the expedition included several skilled writers, among them Nathaniel Langford. Langford came to Montana during the gold rush of 1862 and established a freighting business and a saw mill. He was appointed as federal tax collector but resigned that position to accept an appointment as territorial governor; however, the Senate refused to confirm him.

Langford describes a meeting on September 9 in which

members of the party came up with the idea of creating a national park, a story that has become deeply embedded in Yellowstone mythology. Despite its appeal, many historians doubt the tale. Paul Schullery and Lee Whittlesey, in their book Myth and History in the Creation of Yellowstone Park, *conclude that the story is "lousy history."*

After the expedition, Nathaniel Langford went on a speaking tour for the Northern Pacific Railroad, which was planning to push track through Montana and was looking for ways to attract riders. In addition to his national tour, Langford wrote two articles that appeared in Scribner's Monthly, *a national magazine that focused on illustration.*

Langford became the first superintendent of Yellowstone National Park, an unpaid position that he held for five years. After he left Yellowstone Park, he returned to his home state of Minnesota where he wrote one book on the Montana vigilantes and another about the Washburn Expedition. Here is an abridged version of his book, The Discovery of Yellowstone Park—Diary of the Washburn Expedition to the Yellowstone and Firehole Rivers in the Year 1870, *which was published in 1905.*

DISCOVERING YELLOWSTONE—1870

Excerpted from Nathaniel Pitt Langford's Diary **of the Washburn Expedition to the Yellowstone and Firehole Rivers in the Year 1870**

Monday, August 22—We are now fairly launched upon our expedition without the possibility of obtaining outside assistance. Means for our protection have been fully considered since we camped, and our plans for guard duty throughout the trip have been arranged. Fresh Indian signs indicate that the redskins are lurking near us, and I am not entirely free from anxiety. Our safety will depend upon our vigilance. We are all well armed with long-range repeating rifles and needle guns, though there are but few of our party who are experts at off-hand shooting with a revolver.

In the course of our discussion Jake Smith expressed his doubt whether any member of our party is sufficiently skilled in the use of the revolver to hit an Indian at even a close range. He offered to put the matter to a test by setting up his hat at a distance of twenty yards for the boys to shoot at with their revolvers at twenty-five cents a shot. While several members of our party were blazing away with indifferent success, with the result that Jake was adding to his exchequer without damage to his hat, I could not resist the inclination to quietly drop out of sight behind a clump of bushes, where from my place of concealment I sent from my breech-loading Ballard bullets in rapid succession, through the hat, badly riddling it.

***N. P. Langford was one of the principal organizers of the
Washburn Expedition, which documented the wonders of the
Upper Yellowstone in 1870. He provided a detailed account
of the group's adventures.***

National Park Service photo by W. H. Jackson, 1871

Jake inquired, "Whose revolver is it that makes that loud report?" He did not discover the true state of the case, but removed the target with the ready acknowledgment that there were members of our party whose aim with a revolver was more accurate than he had thought.

Tuesday, August 23—At 8 a.m. today we broke camp. After some delay occurring in packing our horses, Lieutenant Doane and the escort went ahead, and we did not again see them until we reached our night camp.

Today we saw our first Indians as we descended into the valley of the Yellowstone. They came down from the east side of the valley, over the foothills, to the edge of the plateau overlooking the bottomlands of the river, and there conspicuously displayed themselves for a time to engage our attention. As we passed by them up the valley they moved down to where their ponies were hobbled.

Two of our party, Hauser and Stickney, had dropped behind and passed towards the north to get a shot at an antelope; and when they came up they reported that, while we were observing the Indians on the plateau across the river, there were one hundred or more of them watching us from behind a high butte as our pack-train passed up the valley. As soon as they observed Hauser and Stickney coming up nearly behind them, they wheeled their horses and disappeared down the other side of the butte. This early admonition of our exposure to hostile attack, and liability to be robbed of everything, and compelled on foot and without provisions to retrace our steps, has been the subject of discussion in our camp tonight, and has renewed in our party the determination to abate nothing of our vigilance, and keep in a condition of constant preparation.

With our long-range rifles and plenty of ammunition, we can stand off 200 or 300 of them, with their less efficient weapons, if we don't let them sneak up upon us in the night. If we encounter more than that, then what? The odds will be that they will "rub us out," as Jim Stuart says.

Jake Smith has sent the first demoralizing shot into the camp by announcing that he doesn't think there is any necessity for standing guard. Jake is the only one of our party who shows some sign of baldness, and he probably thinks that his own scalp is not worth the taking by the Indians.

Did we act wisely in permitting him to join our party at the last moment before leaving Helena? One careless man will frequently demoralize an entire company. I think we have now taken all possible precautions for our safety, but our numbers are few. For me to say that I am not in hourly dread of the Indians when they appear in large force would be a braggart boast.

Mr. Everts was taken sick this afternoon. . . .

We have traveled all this day amid this stupendous variety of landscape until we have at length reached the western shore of that vast and solitary river which is to guide us to the theatre of our explorations.

We learn from Mr. Bottler that there are some twenty-five lodges of Crow Indians up the valley.

Wednesday, August 24—It rained nearly all of last night, but Lieutenant Doane pitched his large tent, which was sufficiently capacious to accommodate us all by lying "heads and tails," and we were very comfortable. Throughout the forenoon we had occasional showers, but about noon it cleared away, and we got under way.

Mr. Everts was not well enough to accompany us, and it was arranged that he should remain at Bottler's ranch, and that we would move about twelve miles up the river, and there await his arrival. Our preparations for departure being completed, General Washburn detailed a guard of four men to accompany the pack train, while the rest of the party rode on ahead.

Five miles farther on we crossed a small stream bordered with black cherry trees, many of the smaller ones broken down by bears, of which animal we found many signs. One mile farther on we made our camp about a mile below the middle canyon. Tonight we have antelope, rabbit, duck, grouse and the finest of large trout for supper.

Thursday, August 25—Last night was very cold, the thermometer marking 40 degrees at 8 a.m. At one mile of travel we came to the middle canyon, which we passed on a very narrow trail running over a high spur of the mountain overlooking the river, which at this point is forced through a narrow gorge, surging and tumbling and boiling over the rocks, the water having a dark green color. After passing the canyon we again left the valley, passing over the mountain.

At nineteen miles from our morning camp we came to Gardiner's River, at the mouth of which we camped. Mr. Everts came into camp just at night, nearly recovered, but very tired from his long and tedious ride over a rugged road, making our two days' travel in one. Along our trail of today are plenty of Indian "signs" and marks of the lodge poles dragging in the sand on either side of the trail.

Jake Smith stood guard last night, or ought to have done so, and but for the fact that Gillette was also on guard, I should not have had an undisturbed sleep. We know that the Indians are near us, and sleep is more refreshing to me when I feel assured that I will not be joined in my slumbers by those who are assigned for watchful guard duty.

Friday, August 26—For some reason we did not leave camp till 11 o'clock. We forded Gardiner's river with some difficulty, several of our pack animals being nearly carried off their feet by the torrent. In the morning Lieutenant Doane and one of his men, together with Mr. Everts, had started out ahead of the party to search out the best trail. At 3 o'clock we arrived at Antelope creek, only six miles from our morning camp, where we concluded to halt. On the trail that we were following there were no tracks except those of unshod ponies; and, as our horses were all shod, it was evident that Lieutenant Doane and the advance party had descended the mountain by some other trail than that which we were following.

Our camp tonight is on Antelope creek, about five miles from the Yellowstone River. After our arrival in camp, in company with Stickney and Gillette, I made a scout of eight or ten miles through the country east of our trail, and between it and the river, in search of some sign of Lieutenant Doane, but we found no trace of him. We could discern the trail for many miles on its tortuous course, but could see no sign of a camp, or of horses feeding, and we returned to our camp.

Saturday, August 27—I have appropriated a sack of beans to sit on; and, as Hedges and I have been writing, there has been a lively game of cards played near my left side, which Hedges, who has just closed his diary, says is a game of poker. I doubt if Deacon Hedges is sufficiently posted in the game to know to a certainty that poker is the game which is being played; but, putting what Hedges tells me with what I see and hear, I find that these infatuated players have put a valuation of five cents per bean, on beans that did not cost more than $1 a quart in Helena. Jake Smith exhibits a marvelous lack of veneration for his kinswoman, by referring to each bean, as he places it before him upon the table, as his "aunt," or, more flippantly, his "auntie."

Walter Trumbull has been styled the "Banker," and he says that at the commencement of the game he sold forty of these beans to each of the players, himself included (200 in all), at five cents each. He has already redeemed the entire 200 at that rate, and now Jake Smith has a half-pint cup nearly full of beans, and is demanding of Trumbull that he redeem them also, that is, pay five cents per bean for the contents of the cup. Trumbull objects. Jake persists. Reflecting upon their disagreement I recall that about an hour ago Jake, with an apologetic "Excuse me!" disturbed me while I was writing and untied the bean sack on which I am now sitting, and took from it a double handful of beans.

It seems to me that a game of cards which admits of such latitude as this, with a practically unlimited draft upon outside resources, is hardly fair to all parties, and especially to "The Banker."

Sunday, August 28—Today being Sunday, we remained all day in our camp, which Washburn and Everts have named "Camp Comfort," as we have an abundance of venison and trout.

We visited the falls of the creek, the waters of which tumble over the rocks and boulders for the distance of 200 yards from our camp, and then fall a distance of 110 feet, as triangulated by Mr. Hauser. Stickney ventured to the verge of the fall, and, with a stone attached to a strong cord, measured its height, which he gives as 105 feet.

The stream, in its descent to the brink of the fall, is separated into half a dozen distorted channels, which have zigzagged their passage through the cement formation, working it into spires, pinnacles, towers and many other capricious objects. Many of these are of faultless symmetry, resembling the minaret of a mosque. . . .

The scenery here cannot be called grand or magnificent, but it is most beautiful and picturesque. The spires are from 75 to 100 feet in height.

In camp today several names were proposed for the creek and fall. At the outset of our journey we had agreed that we would not give to any object of interest that we might discover the name of any of our party nor of our friends. This rule was to be religiously observed. Walter Trumbull suggested "Minaret Creek" and "Minaret Fall." Mr. Hauser suggested "Tower Creek" and "Tower Fall." After some discussion a vote was taken, and by a small majority, the name "Minaret" was decided upon.

During the following evening Mr. Hauser stated with great seriousness that we had violated the agreement made relative to naming objects for our friends. He said that the well known Southern family—the Rhetts—lived in St. Louis, and that they had a most charming and accomplished daughter named "Minnie." He said that this daughter was a sweetheart of Trumbull, who had proposed the name— her name, "Minnie Rhett"—and that we had unwittingly given to the fall and creek the name of this sweetheart of Mr. Trumbull.

Mr. Trumbull indignantly denied the truth of Hauser's statement, and Hauser as determinedly insisted that it was the truth. The vote was therefore reconsidered, and by a substantial majority it was decided to substitute the name "Tower" for "Minaret." Later, and when it was too late to recall or reverse the action of our party, it was surmised that Hauser himself had a sweetheart in St. Louis—a Miss Tower.

Monday, August 29—We broke camp about 8 o'clock, leaving the trail, which runs down to the mouth of the creek, and passed over a succession of high ridges, and part of the time through fallen timber.

Toiling on our course down this creek to the river we came suddenly upon a basin of boiling sulphur springs, exhibiting signs of activity and points of difference so wonderful as to fully absorb our curiosity. The largest of these, about twenty feet in diameter, is boiling like a cauldron. Its appearance has suggested the name "Hell-Broth Springs." Around them all is an incrustation formed from the bases of the spring deposits, arsenic, alum, sulphur, etc.

This incrustation is sufficiently strong in many places to bear the weight of a man, but more frequently it gave way, and from the apertures thus created hot steam issued, showing it to be dangerous to approach the edge of the springs; and it was with the greatest difficulty that I obtained specimens of the incrustation. This I finally accomplished by lying at full length upon that portion of the incrustation which yielded the least, but which was not sufficiently strong to bear my weight while I stood upright. At imminent risk of sinking in the infernal mixture, I rolled over and over to the edge of the opening; and, with the crust slowly bending and sinking beneath me, hurriedly secured the coveted prize of black sulphur, and rolled back to a place of safety.

It was again Jake Smith's turn for guard duty last night, but this morning Jake's countenance wore a peculiar expression, which indicated that he possessed some knowledge not shared by the rest of the party. He spoke never a word, and was as serene as a Methodist minister behind four aces. My interpretation of this self-satisfied serenity is that his guard duty did not deprive him of much sleep. In a matter in which the safety of our whole party is involved, it is unfortunate that there are no "articles of war" to aid in the enforcement of discipline, in faithful guard duty.

Tuesday, August 30—When we left our camp this morning at Hell-Broth Springs, I remarked to Mr. Hedges and General Washburn that the wonders of which we were in pursuit had not disappointed us in their first exhibitions. When we reached Cascade creek, on which we are now encamped, after a short day of journeying, it was with much astonishment as well as delight that we found ourselves in the immediate presence of the falls. Their roar, smothered by the vast depth of the canyon into which they plunge, was not heard until they were before us. With remarkable deliberation we unsaddled and lariated our horses, and even refreshed ourselves with such creature comforts as our larder readily afforded, before we deigned a survey of these great wonders of nature.

We have decided to remain at this point through the entire day tomorrow, and examine the canyon and falls. From the brief survey of the canyon I was enabled to make before darkness set in, I am impressed with its awful grandeur, and I realize the impossibility of giving to anyone who has not seen a gorge similar in character any idea of it.

It is getting late, and it is already past our usual bedtime, and Jake Smith is calling to me to "turn in" and give him a chance to sleep. There is in what I have already seen so much of novelty to fill the mind and burden the memory, that unless I write down in detail the events of each day, and indeed almost of each hour as it passes, I shall not be able to prepare for publication on my return home any clear or satisfactory account of these wonders. I will write until my candle burns out. Jacob is indolent and fond of slumber, and I think that he resents my remark to him the other day, that he could burn more and gather less wood than any man I ever camped with. He has dubbed me "The Yellowstone sharp." Good! I am not ashamed to have the title.

Wednesday, August 31—This has been a "red-letter" day with me, and one that I shall not soon forget, for my mind is clogged and my memory confused by what I have today seen. General Washburn and Mr. Hedges are sitting near me, writing, and we have an understanding that we will compare our notes when finished. We are all overwhelmed with astonishment and wonder at what we have seen, and we feel that we have been near the very presence of the Almighty.

The place where I obtained the best and most terrible view of the canyon was a narrow projecting point situated two or three miles below the lower fall. Standing there or rather lying there for greater safety, I thought how utterly impossible it would be to describe to another the sensations inspired by such a presence.

The two grand falls of the Yellowstone form a fitting completion to this stupendous climax of wonders. The upper fall, as determined by the rude means of measurement at our command, is one hundred and fifteen feet in height. The river approaches it through a passage of rocks, which rise one hundred feet on either side above its surface.

Very beautiful as is this fall, it is greatly excelled in grandeur and magnificence by the cataract half a mile below it, where the river takes another perpendicular plunge of three hundred and twenty feet into the most gloomy cavern that ever received so majestic a visitant. The fall itself takes its leap between the jaws of rocks whose vertical height above it is more than six hundred feet, and more than nine hundred feet above the chasm into which it falls. Long before it reaches the base, it is enveloped in spray, which is woven by the sun's rays into bows radiant with all the colors of the prism.

Thursday, September 1—If we had not decided, last night, that we would move on today, I think that every member of the party would have been glad to stay another day at the canyon and falls. I will, however, except out of the number our comrade Jake Smith. The afternoon of our arrival at the canyon (day before yesterday), after half an hour of inspection of the falls and canyon, he said: "Well, boys, I have seen all there is, and I am ready to move on."

However, the perceptible decline in our larder, and the uncertainty of the time to be occupied in further explorations, forbid more than these two days' stay at the falls and canyon. . . .

Six miles above the upper fall we entered upon a region remarkable for the number and variety of its hot springs and craters. The principal spring, and the one that first meets the eye as you approach from the north, is a hot sulphur spring, of oval shape, the water of which is constantly boiling and is thrown up to the height of from three to seven feet. The moistened bed of a dried-up rivulet, leading from the edge of the spring down inside through this deposit, showed us that the spring had but recently been overflowing. Farther along the base of this mountain is a sulphurous cavern about twenty feet deep, and seven or eight feet in diameter at its mouth, out of which the steam is thrown in jets with a sound resembling the puffing of a steam-boat when laboring over a sand-bar, and with as much uniformity and intonation as if emitted by a high-pressure engine. From hundreds of fissures in the adjoining mountain from base to summit, issue hot sulphur vapors, the apertures through which they escape being encased in thick incrustations of sulphur, which in many instances is perfectly pure. There are nearby a number of small sulphur springs, not especially remarkable in appearance.

The tramp of our horses' feet as we rode over the incrustation at the base of the mountain returned a hollow sound; yet while some of our party were not disposed to venture upon it with their horses, still I think with care in selecting a route there is very little danger in riding over it.

Five miles further on we camped near the "Mud Geyser." Our course today has been for the greater part over a level valley, which was plainly visible from the top of Mount Washburn. The water of the river at this point is strongly impregnated with the mineral bases of the springs surrounding our camp, and that empty into the river above it.

Friday, September 2—Today we have occupied ourselves in examining the springs and other wonders at this point. At the base of the foot-hills adjoining our camp are three large springs of thick boiling mud, the largest of which resembles an immense cauldron. It is about thirty feet in diameter, bordered by a rim several feet wide, upon which one can stand within reach of the boiling mass of mud. Its surface is four or five feet below the rim enclosing it, the rim being a little raised above the surrounding level. From these we passed over the timbered hill at the base of which these springs are situated. In the timber along the brow of the hill and near its summit, and immediately under the living trees, the hot sulphur vapor and steam issue from several fissures or craters, showing that the hottest fires are raging at some point beneath the surface crust, which in a great many places gives forth a hollow sound as we pass over it. . . .

While surveying these wonders, our ears were constantly saluted by dull, thundering, booming sounds, resembling the reports of distant artillery. As we approached the spot whence they proceeded, the ground beneath us shook and trembled as from successive shocks of an earthquake. Ascending a small hillock, the cause of the uproar was found to be a mud volcano—the greatest marvel we have yet met with. It is about midway up a gentle pine-covered slope, above which on the lower side its crater, thirty feet in diameter, rises to a height of about thirty-five feet. Dense masses of steam issue with explosive force from this crater, into whose tapering mouth, as they are momentarily dispelled by the wind, we can see at a depth of about forty feet the regurgitating contents. The explosions are not uniform in force or time, varying from three to eight seconds, and occasionally with perfect regularity occurring every five seconds. They are very distinctly heard at the distance of half a mile, and the massive jets of vapor which accompany them burst forth like the smoke of burning gunpowder.

We did not dare to stand upon the leeward side of the crater and withstand the force of the steam; and Mr. Hedges, having ventured too near the rim on that side, endangered his life by his temerity, and was thrown violently down the exterior side of the crater by the force of the volume of steam emitted during one of these fearful convulsions. General Washburn and I, who saw him fall, were greatly concerned lest while regaining his feet, being blinded by the steam, and not knowing in which direction to turn, he should fall into the crater.

From the mud volcano we moved up the valley about four miles to our camp on the river, passing several mud puffs on the way.

Saturday, September 3—Yellowstone lake, as seen from our camp tonight, seems to me to be the most beautiful body of water in the world. In front of our camp it has a wide sandy beach like that of the ocean, which extends for miles and as far as the eye can reach, save that occasionally there is to be found a sharp projection of rocks. The overlooking bench rises from the water's edge about eight feet, forming a bank of sand or natural levee, which serves to prevent the overflow of the land adjoining, which, when the lake is receiving the water from the mountain streams that empty into it while the snows are melting, is several feet below the surface of the lake. On the shore of the lake, within three or four miles of our camp, are to be found specimens of sandstone, resembling clay, of sizes varying from that of a walnut to a flour barrel, and of every odd shape imaginable. Fire and water have been at work here together—fire to throw out the deposit in a rough shape, and water to polish it.

From our camp we can see several islands from five to ten miles distant in a direct line. Two of the three "Tetons," which are so plainly visible to travelers going to Montana from Eagle Rock bridge on Snake River, and which are such well-known and prominent landmarks on that stage route, we notice tonight in the direction of south 25 degrees west from our camp. We shall be nearer to them on our journey around the lake.

Sunday, September 4—This morning at breakfast time Lieutenant Doane was sleeping soundly and snoring sonorously, and we decided that we would not waken him, but would remain in camp till the afternoon and perhaps until morning. Walter Trumbull suggested that a proper deference to Jake Smith's religious sentiments ought to be a sufficient reason for not traveling on Sunday, whereupon Jake immediately exclaimed, "If we're going to remain in camp, let's have a game of draw."

Monday, September 5—We came to camp on the shore of the lake, after having marched fifteen miles in a southerly direction. We have a most beautiful view of the lake from our camp.

Tonight a conference of the party was held to decide whether we would continue our journey around the lake, or retrace our steps and pass along the north side of the lake over to the Madison. By a vote of six to three we have decided to go around the lake. Mr. Hauser voted in favor of returning by way of the north side. My vote was cast for going around the lake.

As we passed along the shore today, we could see the steam rising from a large group of hot springs on the opposite shore of the lake bordering on what seems to be the most westerly bay or estuary. We will have an opportunity to examine them at short range when we have completed our journey around the lake.

Tuesday, September 6—We broke camp at ten thirty this morning, bearing well to the southeast for an hour and then turning nearly due south, our trail running through the woods, and for a large part of our route throughout the day, through fallen timber, which greatly impeded our progress. We did not make over ten miles in our day's travel. Frequently we were obliged to leave the trail running through the woods, and return to the lake, and follow the beach for some distance.

Wednesday, September 7—Last night when all but the guards were asleep, we were startled by a mountain lion's shrill scream, sounding so like the human voice that for a moment I was deceived by it into believing that some traveler in distress was hailing our camp.

Thursday, September 8—Our journey for the entire day has been most trying, leading us through a trackless forest of pines encumbered on all sides by prostrate trunks of trees. The difficulty of urging forward our pack train, making choice of routes, extricating the horses when wedged between the trees, and readjusting the packs so that they would not project beyond the sides of the horses, required constant patience and untiring toil. The struggle between our own docility and the obstacles in our way, not infrequently resulted in fits of sullenness or explosions of wrath, which bore no slight resemblance to the volcanic forces of the country itself.

One of our pack horses is at once a source of anxiety and amusement to us all. He is a remarkable animal owned by Judge Hedges, who, however, makes no pretentions to being a good judge of horses. Mr. Hedges says that the man from whom he purchased the animal, in descanting upon his many excellent qualities, said: "He is that kind of an animal that drives the whole herd before him." The man spoke truly, but Mr. Hedges did not realize that the seller meant to declare that the animal, from sheer exhaustion, would always be lagging behind the others of the herd. From the start, and especially during our journey through the forest, this pony, by his acrobatic performances and mishaps, has furnished much amusement for us all. Progress today could only be accomplished by leaping our animals over the fallen trunks of trees. Our little bronco, with all the spirit necessary, lacks oftentimes the power to scale the tree trunks. As a consequence, he is frequently found resting upon his midriff with his fore and hind feet suspended over the opposite sides of some huge log. "The spirit indeed is willing, but the flesh is weak." He has an ambitious spirit, which is exceeded only by his patience. He has had many mishaps, any one of which would have permanently disabled a larger animal, and we have dubbed him "Little Invulnerable."

Friday, September 9—We broke camp this morning with the pack train at 10 o'clock, traveling in a westerly course for about two miles, when we gradually veered around to a nearly easterly direction, through fallen timber almost impassable in the estimation of pilgrims, and indeed pretty severe on our pack horses, for there was no trail.

Frequently, we were obliged to rearrange the packs and narrow them, so as to admit of their passage between the standing trees. At one point the pack animals became separated, and with the riding animals of a portion of the party were confronted with a prostrate trunk of a huge tree, about four feet in diameter, around which it was impossible to pass because of the obstructions of fallen timber. Yet pass it we must; and the animals, one after another, were brought up to the log, their breasts touching it, when Williamson and I, the two strongest men of the party, on either side of an animal, stooped down, and, placing each a shoulder back of a fore leg of a horse, rose to an erect position, while others of the party placed his fore feet over the log, which he was thus enabled to scale. In this way we lifted fifteen or twenty of our animals over the log.

Soon after leaving our camp this morning our "Little Invulnerable," while climbing a steep rocky ascent, missed his footing and turned three back summersaults down into the bottom of the ravine. We assisted him to his feet without removing his pack, and he seemed none the worse for his adventure, and quickly regained the ridge from which he had fallen and joined the rest of the herd.

At 3 o'clock in the afternoon we halted for the day, having traveled about six miles, but our camp tonight is not more than three miles from our morning camp.

"Little Invulnerable" was missing when we camped; and, as I was one of the four men detailed for the day to take charge of the pack train, I returned two miles on our trail with the two packers, Reynolds and Bean, in search of him. We found him wedged between two trees, evidently enjoying a rest, which he sorely needed after his remarkable acrobatic feat of the morning.

We are camped in a basin not far from the lake, which

surrounds us on three sides—east, north and west. Mr. Everts has not yet come into camp, and we fear that he is lost.

Last night we had a discussion—growing out of the fact that Hedges and Stickney, for a brief time, were lost—for the purpose of deciding what course we would adopt in case any other member of the party were lost. We agreed that in such case we would all move on as rapidly as possible to the southwest arm of the lake, where there are hot springs (the vapor of which we noticed from our camp of September 5th), and there remain until all the party were united. Everts thought a better way for a lost man would be to strike out nearly due west, hoping to reach the headwaters of the Madison River, and follow that stream as his guide to the settlements; but he finally abandoned this idea and adopted that which has been approved by the rest of the party. So if Mr. Everts does not come into camp tonight, we will tomorrow start for the appointed rendezvous.

Saturday, September 10—We broke camp about 10 o'clock this morning, taking a course of about ten degrees north of west, traveling seven miles, and coming to camp on the lakeshore at about five miles in a direct line from our morning camp at half past two p.m. No sign of Mr. Everts has been seen today, and, on our arrival in camp, Gillette and Trumbull took the return track upon the shore of the lake, hoping to find him, or discover some sign of him. A large fire was built on a high ridge commanding all points on the beach, and we fired signal guns from time to time throughout the night.

Mr. Hauser and I ascended a high point overlooking our camp, and on this high point built a large fire which could be seen for many miles in all directions by anyone not under the bank of the lake, and which we hoped Mr. Everts might see, and so be directed to our camp.

We are more than ever anxious about Mr. Everts. We had hoped, this morning, to make our camp tonight on the southwest arm of the lake, but the fallen timber has delayed us in our travel and prevented our doing so. The southwest arm of the lake has been our objective point for the past three days, and we feel assured that Mr. Everts, finding himself lost, will press on for that point, and, as he will not be hindered by the care of a pack train, he can travel twice as far in one day as we can, and we are therefore the more anxious to reach our destination. We have carefully considered all the points in the case, and have unanimously decided that it will be utter folly to remain in camp here, and equally so to have remained in this morning's camp, hoping that he would overtake us.

Sunday, September 11—Gillette and Trumbull returned to camp this morning, having traversed the shore of the lake to a point east of our camp of September 9th, without discovering any sign of Mr. Everts. We have arrived at the conclusion that he has either struck out for the lake on the west, or followed down the stream which we crossed the day he was lost, or that he is possibly following us. The latter, however, is not very probable.

Mr. Hauser, Lieutenant Doane, and I saddled up immediately after breakfast, and, with a supply of provisions for Mr. Everts, pressed forward in advance of the rest of the party, marking a trail for the pack animals through the openings in the dense woods, and avoiding, as far as possible, the fallen timber. We rode through with all possible dispatch, watching carefully for the tracks of a horse.

The pack train arrived early in the afternoon with the rest of the party, and all were astonished and saddened that no trace of Mr. Everts had been found. We shall tonight mature a plan for a systematic search for him. It is probable that we will make this camp the base of operations, and remain here several days. Everts has with him a supply of matches, ammunition, and fishing tackle, and if he will but travel in a direct line and not veer around to the right or left in a circle, he will yet be all right.

We were roused this morning about 2 o'clock by the shrill howl of a mountain lion, and again while we were at breakfast we heard another yell. As we stood around our campfire tonight, our ears were saluted with a shriek so terribly human, that for a moment we believed it to be a call from Mr. Everts, and we hallooed in response, and several of our party started in the direction whence the sounds came, and would have instituted a search for our comrade but for an admonitory growl of a mountain lion.

We have traveled today about seven miles. On leaving our camps yesterday and today, we posted conspicuously at each a placard, stating clearly the direction we had taken and where provisions could be found.

Monday, September 12—In accordance with our prearranged program, three parties were sent out this morning in search of Mr. Everts. Smith and Trumbull were to follow the lake shore until they came in sight of our last camp. Hauser and Gillette were to return on our trail through the woods, taking with them their blankets and two days' rations. General Washburn and myself were to take a southerly direction towards what we called "Brown Mountain," some twelve miles away. Smith and Trumbull returned early in the afternoon and reported having seen in the sand the tracks of a man's foot, and Smith thought that he saw several Indians, who disappeared in the woods as they approached; but Trumbull, who was with him, did not see them, and Smith says it was because he was short-sighted. For some reason they did not pursue their investigations farther, and soon returned in good order to camp.

The reconnaissance made by General Washburn and myself resulted in no discovery of any trace of Everts. We traveled about eleven miles directly south, nearly to the base of Brown Mountain, carefully examining the ground the whole of the way, to see if any horseshoe tracks could be discovered. We crossed no stream between the lake and the mountain, and if Mr. Everts followed the stream which we crossed on the 9th, he is south of Brown Mountain, for it is evident that he did not pass westward between Brown

Mountain and Yellowstone Lake; otherwise we would have discovered the tracks of his horse.

It is now night, and Hauser and Gillette have not yet returned.

Two miles on this side (the north side) of Brown Mountain, Washburn and I passed over a low divide, which, I think, must be the main range of the Rocky Mountains, just beyond which is another brimstone basin containing forty or fifty boiling sulphur and mud springs, and any number of small steam jets. A small creek runs through the basin, and the slopes of the mountains on either side to the height of several hundred feet showed unmistakable signs of volcanic action beneath the crust over which we were traveling. A considerable portion of the slope of the mountain was covered with a hollow incrustation of sulphur and lime, or silica, from which issued in many places hot steam, and we found many small craters from six to twelve inches in diameter, from which issued the sound of the boiling sulphur or mud, and in many instances we could see the mud or sulphur water. There are many other springs of water slightly impregnated with sulphur, in which the water was too hot for us to bear the hand more than two or three seconds, and which overflowed the green spaces between the incrustations, completely saturating the ground, and over which in many places the grass had grown, forming a turf compact and solid enough to bear the weight of a man ordinarily; but when it once gave way the underlying deposit was so thin that it afforded no support.

While crossing, heedless of General Washburn's warning, my horse broke through one of these green places and sank to his body as if in a bed of quicksand. I was off his back in an instant and succeeded in extricating the struggling animal, the turf being strong enough to bear his body alone, without the addition of the weight of a man. The fore legs of my horse, however, had gone through the turf into the hot, thin mud beneath. General Washburn, who was a few yards behind me on an incrusted mound of lime and sulphur (which bore us in all cases), and who had just before called to me to keep off the grassy place, as there was danger beneath it, inquired of me if the deposit beneath the turf was hot. Without making examination I answered that I thought it might be warm. Shortly afterwards the turf again gave way, and my horse plunged more violently than before, throwing me over his head, and, as I fell, my right arm was thrust violently through the treacherous surface into the scalding morass, and it was with difficulty that I rescued my poor horse, and I found it necessary to instantly remove my glove to avoid blistering my hand. The frenzied floundering of my horse had in the first instance suggested to General Washburn the idea that the under stratum was hot enough to scald him. General Washburn was right in his conjecture. It is a fortunate circumstance that I today rode my lightweight packhorse; for, if I had ridden my heavy saddle horse, I think that the additional weight of his body would have broken the turf that held up the lighter animal and he would have disappeared in the hot boiling mud, taking me with him.

Mr. Stickney has today made an inventory of our larder, and we find that our luxuries, such as coffee, sugar and flour, are nearly used up, and that we have barely enough of necessary provisions—salt, pepper, etc., to last us ten days longer. We will remain at the lake probably three or four days longer with the hope of finding some trace of Everts, when it will be necessary to turn our faces homewards to avoid general disaster. In the meantime we will dry a few hundred pounds of trout, and carry them with us as a precautionary measure against starvation.

At all of our camps for the past three days, and along the line of travel between them, we have blazed the trees as a guide for Mr. Everts, and have left a small supply of provisions at each place, securely cached, with notices directing Mr. Everts to the places of concealment. The soldiers' rations issued for thirty days' service will barely hold out for their own use, and we have little chance of borrowing from them. We left Helena with thirty days' rations, expecting to be absent but twenty-five days. We have already been journeying twenty-seven days, and are still a long way from home.

Tuesday, September 13—We have remained in camp all day. At about 9 o'clock this morning it began to rain and hail, and we have had a little snow, which continued to fall at intervals all day. At about 6 o'clock this evening Hauser and Gillette arrived in camp, having returned on the trail to within three miles of the place where we camped on the night of September 7th. They examined the trail and the beach with the utmost care, but without discovering any trace of Mr. Everts. They say that the trail over which our train passed, or, rather, the path which our train made, was hardly plain enough to be followed, and in many places where the pine leaves had fallen thick upon the ground, it was totally invisible, so that no one could have followed it with certainty except by dismounting and closely observing the ground at every step. They made the journey very well, from the fact that they had traveled the route once before, and their horses instinctively followed the back path for a great part of the distance without any special guidance. On their near approach to camp, when the trail was no longer discernible, their dog "Booby" took the lead when they were at fault, and brought them into camp all right. They think they might have been forced to lie out all night but for the sagacity of Booby. They made on each of the two days nearly as great a distance as our train traveled in four days. Their report has fully set at rest the question of Mr. Everts having followed us. It settles as a fact that he did not again strike our trail, and that had he done so he could not have followed it, owing to his shortsightedness. Hauser and Gillette are probably the two best trailers and woodsmen in our party, and their report of the condition of the trail and the difficulty experienced in following it has satisfied us that Mr. Everts has either struck off in a southerly direction, following perhaps the headwaters of the Snake River, or that he has made an effort to reach the head of the lake with a view of returning by our trail to Bottler's ranch. It is snowing hard tonight, and the prospect for a day or two more in this camp is very good. The murky atmosphere tonight brings to view a number of springs on the opposite shore of this arm of the lake and farther back in the hills, which we have not heretofore seen, and the steam is rising from fifty craters in the timbered ridge, giving it the appearance of a New England factory village.

After holding a council this evening we have resolved to remain at this place two days more, hoping that Mr. Everts may overtake us, this arm of the lake being the objective point of our travel, fixed on the day before that on which Mr. Everts was lost.

Wednesday, September 14—We have remained in camp all day, as it is next to impossible to move. The snow is nearly two feet deep, and is very wet and heavy, and our horses are pawing in it for forage. Our large army tent is doing us good service, and, as there is an abundance of dry wood close by our camp, we are extremely comfortable. I am the only one of the party who has a pair of waterproof boots, and I was up and out of the tent this morning before daylight cutting into cordwood a pine log, and before noon I had more than a half cord at the tent door. Washburn and Hauser offered to do some of this work if I would loan them my waterproof boots; but, as they are of a full size for me, and would probably drop off of their feet, I told them that I would get the wood.

Thursday, September 15—This forenoon the weather moderated, and one-half the snow has melted, so that it is but about ten inches deep tonight. Still, our horses are becoming restless for want of sufficient food.

Each night that we have been camped here we have heard the shrill cries of the mountain lions, and under a momentary illusion I have each time been half convinced that it was a human being in distress. Because of the mountain lions, we are keeping close watch upon our horses. They are very fond of horseflesh, and oftentimes will follow a horseman a long distance, more to make a meal upon the flesh of the horse than for the purpose of attacking the rider.

Friday, September 16—We this morning resolved to move over to the vicinity of the hot springs on the opposite side of this arm of the lake, from which point we will leave the Yellowstone for the Madison River or some one of its branches.

These springs surpass in extent, variety, and beauty any that we have heretofore seen. They extend for the distance of nearly a mile along the shore of the lake, and back from the beach about one hundred yards. They number between ninety and one hundred springs, of all imaginable varieties.

Our explorations of the Yellowstone will cease at this point, and tomorrow we start in our search for Firehole Basin. Our journey around Yellowstone Lake in close proximity to the beach is doubtless the first ever attempted; and, although it has been attended with difficulty and distress, these have been to me as nothing, compared with the enjoyment the journey has afforded, and it is with the greatest regret that I turn my face from it homewards. How can I sum up its wonderful attractions! It is dotted with islands of great beauty, as yet unvisited by man, but which at no remote period will be adorned with villas and the ornaments of civilized life. The winds from the mountain gorges roll its placid waters into a furious sea, and crest its billows with foam. Forests of pine, deep, dark and almost impenetrable, are scattered at random along its banks, and its beautiful margin presents every variety of sand and pebbly beach, glittering with crystals, carnelians, and chalcedony. The Indians approach it under the fear of a superstition originating in the volcanic forces surrounding it, which amounts almost to entire exclusion. It possesses adaptabilities for the highest display of artificial culture, amid the greatest wonders of Nature that the world affords, and is beautified by the grandeur of the most extensive mountain scenery, and not many years can elapse before the march of civil improvement will reclaim this delightful solitude and garnish it with all the attractions of cultivated taste and refinement.

It is a source of great regret to us all that we must leave this place and abandon the search for Mr. Everts; but our provisions are rapidly diminishing, and force of circumstances obliges us to move forward. We still indulge the hope that he may have found and followed down some branch of the Madison River and reached Virginia City, or down Snake River and reached some settlement in that valley. But for our anxiety to reach home and prove or disprove our expectations, we might have devoted much more time to visiting the objects of interest we have seen and which we have been obliged to pass by.

Saturday, September 17—This has been a gloomy morning in our camp, for we all have been depressed at the thought of leaving the lake and abandoning the search for Mr. Everts.

We have discussed the situation from every point of view, and have tried to put ourselves in his place and have considered all the possibilities of fate that may befall him. At one moment he may be buoyed up with hope, however faint—at another weighed down by despair and fear, with all their mental terrors. Has he met death by accident, or may he be injured and unable to move, and be suffering the horrors of starvation and fever? Has he wandered aimlessly hither and thither until bereft of reason? As I contemplate all these possibilities, it is a relief to think that he may have lost his life at the hand of some vagabond Indian.

As the result of this conference we have decided upon a final plan of action. We will give to Gillette from our remnant of provisions (ten days' rations) and Lieutenant Doane will detail Privates Moore and Williamson, with ten days' rations, and the three will continue the search from this point. Mr. Gillette says that with the ten days' rations they can devote five days to a continuous search, and the remaining five days will be sufficient, with forced traveling, for them to overtake us.

Hauser has endeavored to throw a little cheer into the conference by saying to Gillette: "I think that I should be willing to take the risk of spending ten days more in this wilderness, if I thought that by so doing I could find a father-in-law." This provoked an uproarious shout of laughter, for we well understood that Hauser alluded to the many social courtesies which Gillette, in Helena, had extended to Miss Bessie Everts, the charming daughter of our lost comrade, and one of the most attractive of Montana belles.

Saturday, September 17, evening—Gillette, Moore and Williamson left us this morning about 9 o'clock on their final quest for Mr. Everts, and the rest of our party soon resumed our journey.

There is still four or five inches of snow on the ground, but there is plenty of long grass under it, and our horses are faring tolerably well, and will soon fill themselves with either grass or snow. There is no clear space large enough for us to pitch our tent. We have had our supper—an indifferent and scanty meal—and each man is now seeking with varied success a dry spot beneath the sheltering branches of the pines whereon to spread his blankets.

Some members of our party, at our early breakfast this morning, sitting upon logs at various distances from our campfire in their half-dried clothing, and eating their scanty meal in silence, presented a sorry appearance. Some are disappointed that we did not, last night, reach the Firehole River, or some large branch of the Madison, which may guide us homeward, and are wondering if we are moving in the right direction. I feel so perfectly confident that we are traveling the right course that I am in the best of spirits. It may be that my cheerfulness is owing, in some degree, to my having dry clothing and a dry skin, which few of my comrades have, but I see no reason for discouragement. I think that Mr. Hauser is the best and most accurate judge of distances, of heights of mountains, and direction of travel, of any man I know, and he does not doubt that we are moving in the right direction. It is a satisfaction to have my opinion confirmed by his judgment.

Sunday, September 18—We left our morning camp about 9 o'clock, pursuing our uncertain course through fallen timber for a distance of about three miles, when we had all our fears of misdirection relieved by coming suddenly upon the banks of the Firehole River, the largest fork of the Madison, down which we followed five miles, passing several groups of boiling springs and a beautiful cascade (to which we gave no name), when we emerged from the dense forest into a sequestered basin two miles above the union of the Firehole River with a stream which comes in from the southwest, the basin extending to the width of a mile, and traversing the river until contracted between proximate ranges two miles below our camp.

I have spent the entire afternoon and part of this evening in examining the geysers and springs, but will not further record the explorations of today until we are ready to leave the basin.

Monday, September 19—When we left Yellowstone Lake two days ago, the desire for home had superceded all thought of further explorations. Five days of rapid travel would, we believed, bring us to the upper valley of the Madison, and within twenty-five miles of Virginia City, and we indulged the remote hope that we might there find some trace of Mr. Everts. We had within a distance of fifty miles seen what we believed to be the greatest wonders on the continent. We were convinced that there was not on the globe another region where within the same limits Nature had crowded so much of grandeur and majesty with so much of novelty and wonder. Judge, then, of our astonishment on entering this basin, to see at no great distance before us an immense body of sparkling water, projected suddenly and with terrific force into the air to the height of over one hundred feet. We had found a real geyser. In the valley before us were a thousand hot springs of various sizes and character, and five hundred craters jetting forth vapor.

We moved down the river on the east bank, part of the way through an open valley and part through fallen timber. At about eight miles we came upon an enormous spring of dark blue water, the largest we have seen. Out near the center of the lake the water boils up a few feet. About one hundred yards from the lake on the side towards the river, the incrustation breaks off perpendicularly, and another large lake is formed, the surface of which is about fifteen feet below the upper and larger lake. There are a few other springs near the river farther down the stream.

Jake Smith, for the first time on this trip, selected at this large lake a curious specimen of tufa. It was a circumstance so unusual that Hedges called our attention to it, but as Smith was riding along holding his treasure carefully in his hand, his horse stumbled, and he accidentally dropped his specimen, and with a remark which I will not here record, and which is at variance with his own Bible instruction, he denounced as worthless all the specimens of the party which he had seen, and inveighed against the folly of spending any time in gathering them.

From this point we passed down the valley close by the bank of the river. The valley on our right was very marshy, and we saw at a considerable distance one very large fountain of water spouting into the atmosphere to a considerable height, and many steam jets, but, owing to the swampy character of the ground, we did not visit them.

When we left Helena on August 17th, we believed that twenty-five days would be the limit of time, which would be consumed before our return; but to meet all exigencies we laid in a thirty days' supply of provisions. We have now been absent thirty-four days, and as we cached some of our supply on Yellowstone Lake for Mr. Everts' relief, we are now on short rations, but the fish we dried while camped on Yellowstone Lake are doing good service.

Tuesday, September 20—We broke camp at half past 9 o'clock, traveling along the rocky edge of the river bank by the rapids, passing thence through a beautiful pine wood and over a long stretch of fallen timber, blackened by fire, for about four miles, when we again reached the river, which here bends in a westerly direction. Lieutenant Doane and I climbed to the top of one of the two prominent hills on our course, and had a fine view of the country for the distance of thirty miles.

Last night, and also this morning in camp, the entire party had a rather unusual discussion. The proposition was made by some member that we utilize the result of our exploration by taking up quarter sections of land at the most prominent points of interest, and a general discussion followed. One member of our party suggested that if there could be secured by pre-emption a good title to two or three quarter sections of land opposite the lower fall of the Yellowstone and extending down the river along the canyon, they would eventually become a source of great profit to the owners. Another member of the party thought that it would be more desirable to take up a quarter section of land at the Upper Geyser Basin, for the reason that that locality could be more easily reached by tourists and pleasure seekers. A third suggestion was that each member of the party pre-empt a claim, and in order that no one should have an advantage over the others, the whole should be thrown into a common pool for the benefit of the entire party.

Mr. Hedges then said that he did not approve of any of these plans—that there ought to be no private ownership of any portion of that region, but that the whole of it ought to be set apart as a great National Park, and that each one of us ought to make an effort to have this accomplished. His suggestion met with an instantaneous and favorable response from all—except one—of the members of our party, and each hour since the matter was first broached, our enthusiasm has increased. It has been the main theme of our conversation today as we journeyed. I lay awake half of last night thinking about it—and if my wakefulness deprived my bedfellow (Hedges) of any sleep, he has only himself and his disturbing National Park proposition to answer for it.

Our purpose to create a park can only be accomplished by untiring work and concerted action in a warfare against the incredulity and unbelief of our national legislators when our proposal shall be presented for their approval. Nevertheless, I believe we can win the battle.

I do not know of any portion of our country where a national park can be established furnishing to visitors more wonderful attractions than here. These wonders are so different from anything we have ever seen—they are so various, so extensive—that the feeling in my mind from the moment they began to appear until we left them has been one of intense surprise and of incredulity. Every day spent in surveying them has revealed to me some new beauty, and now that I have left them, I begin to feel a skepticism which clothes them in a memory clouded by doubt.

Wednesday, September 21—As the outcome of a general conversation tonight, I will leave the party tomorrow morning and start for Virginia City, where I have a forlorn hope that some tidings may be had of Mr. Everts. We think that Virginia City is not more than thirty miles distant; but, as we are not now on any trail leading to it, I shall have to take my chances of finding it.

Jake Smith today asked me if I expected that the readers of my diary would believe what I had written. He said that he had kept no diary for the reason that our discoveries had been of such a novel character, that if he were to write an account of them he would not be believed by those who read his record, and he would be set down as a liar. He said that he did not mind being called a liar by those who had known him well for many years, but he would not allow strangers that privilege. This ambiguous remark indicates that Jake has more wit and philosophy than I have given him the credit of possessing.

Thursday, September 22, Virginia City—With a small supply of needed creature comforts (lunch, etc.), I left the party early this morning, uncertain as to the time, which would be required to take me to Virginia City. About noon I met a horseman who had left Virginia City this morning, who directed me to the trail leading to the town. He paused long enough to let me scan a newspaper, which he had, from which I learned of the capitulation of the French at Sedan. I asked him to hand the newspaper to General Washburn, whose party he would meet in the Madison Valley. He said that he would stop at the cabin of "Bannack George."

The distance from our morning camp to this place is much farther than we thought, and it was 9 o'clock this evening before I reached Virginia City. Nothing has been heard of Mr. Everts, and his friends are shocked at the intelligence of his loss from our party.

Owing to the late hour of my arrival I have met but few of my old acquaintances, but these are greatly interested in the result of our explorations, and I have promised to remain here another day before starting for Helena, and give them a further description of what I have seen.

TRUMAN EVERTS

—ɱ—

Members of the Washburn Expedition spent several days searching for Truman Everts after he disappeared on September 9, 1870, but they had no idea how desperate his plight was. They thought he could always shoot his horse for food if he had to. Only Everts knew that his horse had run away, leaving him with only his clothing and the items in his pockets.

At fifty-one, Everts was by far the oldest member of the expedition and was very nearsighted. Born in Vermont, he returned back east after the expedition, where he fathered a son at the age of seventy-five.

Although he was no outdoorsman, the resourceful Everts found ways to survive by cuddling up to a hot spring during a winter storm and eating thistle roots. More important, he found the will to continue by conjuring an imaginary companion who gave him advice and by arguing with his exhausted arms and feet.

Everts's dramatic story was first published in Scribner's Monthly in 1871 in time to influence the U.S. Congress, which was considering the bill then to established the first national park. It is one of the best known stories in Yellowstone history.

THIRTY-SEVEN PERILOUS DAYS— 1870

From Truman Everts's
story originally published in
Scribner's Monthly *in 1871*

On the day that I found myself separated from the company, our course was impeded by the dense growth of the pine forest. Large tracts of fallen timber frequently rendered our progress almost impossible. Whenever we came to one of these immense windfalls, each man engaged in the pursuit of a passage through it. With the idea that I had found one, I strayed out of sight and hearing of my comrades. As separations like this frequently occurred, it gave me no alarm.

I rode on in the direction, which I supposed had been taken, until darkness overtook me in the dense forest. This was disagreeable enough, but caused me no alarm. I had no doubt of being with the party at breakfast the next morning. I selected a spot for comfortable repose, picketed my horse, built a fire, and went to sleep.

The next morning I rose at early dawn, saddled and mounted my horse, and took my course in the supposed direction of the camp. In searching for the trail I became somewhat confused. The falling foliage of the pines had obliterated every trace of travel. I was obliged frequently to dismount and examine the ground for the faintest indications. Coming to an opening, from which I could see several vistas, I dismounted

Members of the Washburn Expedition searched forests and lakeshores for Truman Everts after he became separated from the party but didn't find him. Everts managed to survive thirty-seven days alone in the Yellowstone Wilderness and gained fame by telling his story.
National Park Service photo by W. H. Jackson, 1871

for the purpose of selecting one leading in the direction I had chosen. Leaving my horse unhitched, I walked a few rods into the forest. While I was surveying the ground my horse took fright, and I turned around in time to see him disappearing at full speed among the trees. That was the last I ever saw of him. My blankets, gun, pistols, fishing tackle, matches—everything, except the clothing on my person, a couple of knives, and a small opera-glass—were attached to the saddle.

I did not yet realize the possibility of a permanent separation from the company. Instead of following up the pursuit of their camp, I engaged in an effort to recover my horse. Half a day's search convinced me of its impracticability.

As the day wore on without any discovery, alarm took the place of anxiety at the prospect of another night alone in the wilderness—this time without food or fire. But even this dismal foreboding was cheered by the hope that I should soon rejoin my companions, who would laugh at my adventure and incorporate it as a thrilling episode into the journal of our trip.

At no time during my period of exile did I experience so much mental suffering from the cravings of hunger as when, exhausted with this long day of fruitless search, I resigned myself to a couch of pine foliage. The forest seemed alive with the screeching of night birds, the angry barking of coyotes, and the prolonged, dismal howl of the gray wolf. These sounds were full of terror, and drove slumber from my eyelids.

Early the next morning I rose unrefreshed. For the first time, I realized that I was lost. Then came a crushing sense of destitution. No food, no fire; no means to procure either; alone in an unexplored wilderness, one hundred and fifty miles from the nearest human abode, surrounded by wild beasts, and famishing with hunger. It was no time for despondency. A moment afterwards I felt how calamity can elevate the mind, in the formation of the resolution "not to perish in that wilderness."

The hope of finding the party still controlled my plans. I thought, by transversing the peninsula centrally, I would be enabled to strike the shore of the lake in advance of their camp, and near the point of departure for the Madison. Acting upon this impression, I rose from a sleepless couch and pursued my way through the timber-entangled forest. A feeling of weakness took the place of hunger. Occasionally, while scrambling over logs and through thickets, a sense of faintness and exhaustion would come over me, but I would suppress it with the audible expression, "This won't do; I must find my company."

Despondency would sometimes strive with resolution for the mastery of my thoughts. Then I would think of home—of my daughter—and of the possible chance of starvation, or death in some more terrible form. But as often as these gloomy forebodings came, I would strive to banish them.

It was mid-day when I emerged from the forest into an open space at the foot of a peninsula. A broad lake of beautiful curvature, with magnificent surroundings, lay before me, glittering in the sunbeams. It was full twelve miles in circumference. A wide belt of sand formed the margin. The ascending vapor from innumerable hot springs, and the sparkling jet of a single geyser, added the feature of novelty to one of the grandest landscapes I ever beheld. The lake was at least one thousand feet lower than the highest point of the peninsula, and several hundred feet below the level of Yellowstone Lake. I gave it the name of Bessie Lake, after the "sole daughter of my house and heart."

Night was fast approaching, and darkness would come with it. While looking for a spot where I might repose in safety, my attention was attracted to a small green plant of so lively a hue as to form a striking contrast with the deep pine foliage. I pulled it up by the root, which was long and tapering, not unlike a radish. It was a thistle. I tasted it; it was palatable and nutritious. My appetite craved it, and the first meal in four days was made on thistle-roots. Eureka! I had found food.

Overjoyed at this discovery, with hunger allayed, I

stretched myself under a tree and fell asleep. How long I slept I know not; but suddenly I was roused by a loud, shrill scream, like that of a human being in distress, poured, seemingly, into the very portals of my ear. There was no mistaking that fearful voice. It was the screech of a mountain lion, so alarmingly near as to cause every nerve to thrill with terror.

I seized with convulsive grasp the limbs of the friendly tree, and swung myself into it. Scrambling hurriedly from limb to limb, I was soon as near the top as safety would permit. The savage beast was snuffing and growling below, apparently on the very spot I had just abandoned.

I answered every growl with a responsive scream. Terrified at the pawing of the beast, I increased my voice to its utmost volume, broke branches from the limbs, and madly hurled them at the spot whence the continued howlings proceeded.

The animal now began to circle the tree, as if to select a spot for springing into it. I shook, with a strength increased by terror, the slender trunk until every limb rustled with the motion. All in vain. The terrible creature pursued his walk around the tree, lashing the ground with his tail, and prolonging his howlings almost to a roar. It was too dark to see, but the movements of the lion kept me apprised of its position.

Whenever I heard it on one side of the tree I speedily changed to the opposite. I would alternately sweat and thrill with horror at the thought of being torn to pieces and devoured by this formidable monster. Expecting at every moment that it would take the deadly leap, I tried to collect my thoughts. Just at this moment it occurred to me that I would try silence.

Clasping the trunk of the tree with both arms, I sat perfectly still. The lion, still filling the forest with the echo of his howlings, suddenly imitated my example. This silence was more terrible than the clatter and crash of his movements through the brushwood. Now I did not know from what direction to expect his attack. Moments passed like hours. After a lapse of time that I cannot estimate, the beast gave a spring into the thicket and ran screaming into the forest.

Had strength permitted, I should have retained my perch till daylight. But with escape from the jaws of the ferocious brute came a sense of overpowering weakness which almost palsied me. Incredible as it may seem, I lay down in my old bed and was soon lost in a slumber.

I did not awake until after daylight. One of those dreary storms of mingled snow and rain, common to these high latitudes, had set in. My clothing, which had been much torn, exposed my person to its "pitiless peltings."

I knew that my escape from the wilderness must be accomplished, if at all, by my own unaided exertions. This thought was terribly afflicting, and brought before me, in vivid array, all the dreadful realities of my condition. I could see no ray of hope. In this condition of mind I could find no better shelter than the spreading branches of a spruce tree, under which, covered with earth and boughs, I lay during the two succeeding days; the storm, meanwhile, raging with unabated violence.

While thus exposed, and suffering from cold and hunger, a little benumbed bird, not larger than a snow-bird, hopped within my reach. I instantly seized and killed it, and, plucking its feathers, ate it raw. It was a delicious meal for a half-starved man.

Taking advantage of a lull in the elements, on the morning of the third day I rose early and started in the direction of a large group of hot springs. The distance I traveled could not have been less than ten miles. Long before I reached the wonderful cluster of natural caldrons, the storm had recommenced. Chilled through, with my clothing thoroughly saturated, I lay down under a tree upon the heated incrustation until completely warmed. My heels and the sides of my feet were frozen.

As soon as warmth had permeated my system, and I had quieted my appetite with a few thistle-roots, I took a survey of my surroundings, and selected a spot between two springs, sufficiently asunder to afford heat at my head and feet. On this spot I built a bower of pine branches, spread its incrusted surface with fallen foliage and small boughs, and stowed myself away to await the close of the storm.

Thistles were abundant, and I had fed upon them long enough to realize that they would, for a while at least, sustain life. In convenient proximity to my abode was a small, round, boiling spring, which I called my dinner-pot, and in which, from time to time, I cooked my roots.

This establishment I occupied seven days—the first three of which were darkened by one of the most furious storms I ever saw. The vapor supplied me with warmth and saturated my clothing. I was enveloped in a perpetual steam-bath.

Nothing gave me more concern than the want of fire. I recalled everything I had ever read or heard of the means by which fire could be produced; but none of them were within my reach. An escape without it was simply impossible.

As I lay in my bower, anxiously awaiting the disappearance of the snow, it occurred to me that I would erect some sort of monument, which might, at some future day, inform a casual visitor of the circumstances under which I had perished. At that moment a gleam of sunshine lit up the bosom of the lake, and with it the thought flashed upon my mind that I could, with a lens from my opera glasses, get fire from heaven. Oh, happy, life-renewing thought!

Instantly subjecting it to the test of experiment when I saw the smoke curl from the bit of dry wood in my fingers, I felt, if the whole world were offered me for it, I would cast it aside before parting with that little spark. I was now the happy possessor of food and fire. These would carry me through. I said to myself, "I will not despair."

My stay at the springs was prolonged several days by an accident that befell me on the third night after my arrival there. An unlucky movement while asleep broke the crust on which I reposed, and the hot steam, pouring upon my hip, scalded it severely before I could escape. This new affliction, added to my frost-bitten feet, already festering, was the cause of frequent delay and unceasing pain through all my wanderings.

After obtaining fire, I set to work making preparations for as early departure as my condition would permit. I had lost both knives since parting from the company, but I now made a convenient substitute by sharpening the tongue of a buckle which I cut from my vest. With this I cut the legs and counters from my boots, making of them a passable pair of slippers, which I fastened to my feet as firmly as I could with strips of bark. With the ravelings of a linen handkerchief, aided by the magic buckle-tongue, I mended my clothing. Of the same material I made a fish-line, which, on finding a piece of red tape in one of my pockets better suited to the purpose, I abandoned as a "bad job." I made of a pin that I found in my coat a fish-hook, and, by sewing up the bottoms of my boot-legs, constructed a very good pair of pouches to carry my food in, fastening them to my belt by the straps.

Thus accoutered, on the morning of the eighth day after my arrival at the springs I bade them a final farewell and started on my course directly across that portion of the neck of the peninsula between me and the southeast arm of Yellowstone Lake. It was a beautiful morning. The sun shone bright and warm, and there was a freshness in the atmosphere truly exhilarating. As I wandered musingly along, the consciousness of being alone, and of having surrendered all hope of finding my friends, returned upon me with crushing power. Weakened by a long fast, and the unsatisfying nature of the only food I could procure, I knew that from this time onward—to the day of my rescue—my mind, though unimpaired in those perceptions needful to self-preservation, was in a condition to receive impressions akin to insanity.

Nevertheless, I was perfectly conscious of the tendency of these morbid influences, and often tried to shake them off. But they would ever return with increased force. I finally reasoned myself into the belief that their indulgence, as it afforded me pleasure, could work no harm while it did not interfere with my plans for deliverance. Thus I lived in a world of ideal happiness, and in a world of positive suffering at the same time.

A change in the wind and an overcast sky, accompanied by cold, brought with them a need of warmth. I drew out my lens and touchwood, but alas! there was no sun. Night, cold, freezing night, set in, and found me exposed to all its terrors. I could only keep from freezing by the most active exertion in walking, rubbing, and striking my benumbed feet and hands against the logs. It seemed the longest, most terrible night of my life, and glad was I when the approaching dawn enabled me to commence retracing my steps to Bessie Lake. I arrived there at noon, built my first fire on the beach, and remained by it, recuperating, for the succeeding two days.

Filling my pouches with thistle-roots, I took a parting survey of the little solitude that had afforded me food and fire the preceding ten days. With something of that melancholy feeling experienced by one who leaves his home to grapple with untried adventures, I started for the nearest point on Yellowstone Lake.

All that day I traveled over timber heaps, amid tree-tops, and through thickets. At noon I took the precaution to obtain fire. With a brand, which I kept alive by frequent blowing and constant waving to and fro, at a late hour in the afternoon, faint and exhausted, I kindled a fire for the night on the only vacant spot I could find amid a dense wilderness of pines. The deep gloom of the forest, in the spectral light revealed on all sides of me a compact and unending growth of trunks, and an impervious canopy of somber foliage; the shrieking of night-birds; the supernaturally human scream of the mountain lion; the prolonged howl of the wolf, made me insensible to all other forms of suffering.

A bright and glorious morning succeeded the dismal night, and brought with it the conviction that I had been the victim of uncontrollable nervous excitement. I resolved henceforth to banish it altogether, and resumed my journey towards the lake.

I doubt if distress and suffering can ever entirely obliterate all sense of natural grandeur and magnificence. Lost in the wonder and admirations inspired by this vast world of beauties, I nearly forgot to improve the few moments of remaining sunshine to obtain fire. With a lighted brand in my hand, I effected a most difficult and arduous descent of the abrupt and stony headland to the beach of the lake.

The sand was soft and yielding. I kindled a fire, and removing the stiffened slippers from my feet attached them to my belt, and wandered barefoot along the sandy shore to gather wood for the night.

The dry, warm sand was most grateful to my lacerated and festering feet, and for a long time after my wood-pile was supplied, I sat with them uncovered. At length conscious of the need of every possible protection from the freezing night atmosphere, I sought my belt for the slippers—and one was missing. I knew I could not travel a day without it.

Fearful that it had dropped into the lake, I searched for an hour among fallen trees and bushes. Success at length rewarded my perseverance. With a feeling of great relief, I now sat down in the sand, my back to a log, and listened to the dash and roar of the waves. It was a wild lullaby, but had no terrors for a worn-out man. I never passed a night of more refreshing sleep.

When I awoke my fire was extinguished save a few embers, which I soon fanned into a cheerful flame. I ate breakfast with some relish, and started along the beach in pursuit of a camp, believing that if successful I should find directions what to do, and food to sustain me. Buoyed by the hope of finding food and counsel, and another night of undisturbed repose in the sand, I resumed my journey along the shore, and at noon found the camp last occupied by my friends on the lake.

A thorough search for food in the ground and trees revealed nothing, and no notice to apprise me of their movements could be seen. A dinner-fork, which afterwards proved to be of infinite service in digging roots, and a yeast-powder can, which would hold half a pint, and which I converted into a drinking-cup and dinner-pot, were the only evidences that the spot had ever been visited by civilized man.

An hour of sunshine in the afternoon enabled me to procure fire, which, in the usual manner, I carried to my camping place. There I built a fire, and to protect myself from the wind, which was blowing violently, lashing the lake into foam, I made a bower of pine boughs, crept under it, and very soon fell asleep.

How long I slept I know not, but I was aroused by the snapping and cracking of the burning foliage, to find my shelter and the adjacent forest in a broad sheet of flame. My left hand was badly burned, and my hair singed closer than a barber would have trimmed it, while I made my escape from the semicircle of burning trees. Among the disasters of this fire, there was none I felt more seriously than the loss of my buckle-tongue knife, my pin fishhook, and tape fish line.

The grandeur of the burning forest surpasses description. An immense sheet of flame, following to their tops the lofty trees of an almost impenetrable pine forest, leaping madly from top to top, and sending thousands of forked tongues a hundred feet or more. Favored by the gale, the conflagration spread with lightning swiftness over an illimitable extent of country—leaving a broad and blackened trail of spectral trunks shorn of limbs and foliage, smoking and burning, to mark the immense sweep of its devastation.

Resolved to search for a trail no longer, when daylight came I selected for a landmark the lowest notch in the Madison Range. Carefully surveying the jagged and broken surface over which I must travel to reach it, I left the lake and pushed into the midst of its intricacies. All the day, until nearly sunset, I struggled over rugged hills, through windfalls, thickets, and matted forests, with the rock-ribbed beacon constantly in view. As I advanced it receded, as if in mockery of my toil.

Night overtook me with my journey half accomplished. The precaution of obtaining fire gave me warmth and sleep, and long before daylight I was on my way. The hope of finding an easy pass into the valley of the Madison inspired me with fresh courage and determination; but long before I arrived at the base of the range, I scanned hopelessly its insurmountable difficulties.

While I was thus considering whether to remain and search for a passage or return to the Yellowstone, I experienced one of those strange hallucinations which many of my friends have misnamed insanity, but which to me was Providence. An old clerical friend, for whose character and counsel I had always cherished peculiar regard, in some unaccountable manner seemed to be standing before me, charged with advice which would relieve my perplexity. I seemed to hear him say, as if in a voice and with the manner of authority, "Go back immediately, as rapidly as your strength will permit. There is no food here, and the idea of scaling these rocks is madness."

"Doctor," I rejoined, "the distance is too great. I cannot live to travel it."

"Say not so. Your life depends upon the effort. Return at once. Start now, lest your resolution falter. Travel as fast and as far as possible—it is your only chance."

"Doctor, I am rejoiced to meet you in this hour of distress, but doubt the wisdom of your counsel. I am within seventy miles of Virginia [City]. Just over these rocks, a few miles away, I shall find friends. My shoes are nearly worn out, my clothes are in tatters, and my strength is almost overcome. As a last trial, it seems to me I can but attempt to scale this mountain or perish in the effort, if God so wills."

"Don't think of it. Your power of endurance will carry you through. I will accompany you. Put your trust in heaven. Help yourself and God will help you."

Overcome by these and other persuasions, and delighted with the idea of having a traveling companion, I plodded my way over the route I had come, intending at a certain point to change it so as to strike the river at the foot of the lake.

Stopping after a few miles of travel, I had no difficulty in procuring fire, and passed a comfortable night. When I resumed my journey the next day the sun was just rising. Whenever I was disposed, as was often the case, to question the wisdom of the change of routes, my old friend appeared to be near with words of encouragement, but his reticence on other subjects both surprised and annoyed me.

Early this day I deflected from my old route and took my course for the foot of the lake, with the hope, by constant travel, to reach it the next day. The distance was greater than I anticipated. Nothing is more deceptive than distance in these high latitudes. At the close of each of the two succeeding days, my point of destination was seemingly as far from me as at the moment I took leave of the Madison Range, and when, cold and hungry, on the afternoon of the fourth day, I had nearly abandoned all hope of escape.

At daybreak I was on the trail down the river. The thought I had adopted from the first—"I will not perish in this wilderness"—often revived my sinking spirits. Once, while struggling through a field of tangled trunks I found myself seriously considering whether it was not preferable to die there than renew the effort to proceed. I felt that all attempt to escape was but a bitter prolongation of the agony of dissolution. A seeming whisper in the air—"While there is life, there is hope; take courage"—broke the delusion, and I clambered on.

I did not forget to use the midday sun to procure fire. Sparks from the lighted brands had burned my hands and crisped the nails of my fingers. The smoke from them had tanned my face to the complexion of an Indian.

While passing through an opening in the forest I found the tip of a gull's wing; it was fresh. I made a fire upon the spot, mashed the bones with a stone, and consigning them to my camp kettle, the yeast-powder box, made half a pint of delicious broth. The remainder of that day and the night ensuing were given to sleep.

I lost all sense of time. Days and nights came and went, numbered only by the growing consciousness that I was gradually starving. I felt no hunger, did not eat to appease appetite, but to renew strength. I experienced but little pain. The gaping sores on my feet, the severe burn on my hip, the festering crevices at the joints of my fingers, all terrible in appearance, had ceased to give me the least concern. The roots which supplied my food had suspended the digestive power of the stomach, and their fibers were packed in it in a matted, compact mass.

Not so with my hours of slumber. They were visited by the most luxurious dreams. I would apparently visit the most gorgeously decorated restaurants of New York and Washington; sit down to immense tables spread with the most appetizing foods; partake of the richest oyster stews and plumpest pies. . . .

It was a cold, gloomy day when I arrived in the vicinity of the falls. The sky was overcast and the snowcapped peaks rose chilly and bleak through the biting atmosphere. The moaning of the wind through the pines, mingling with the sullen roar of the falls, was strangely in unison with my own saddened feelings. I had no heart to gaze upon a scene that a few weeks before had inspired me with rapture and awe. One moment of sunshine was of more value to me but the sun had hid his face and denied me all hope of obtaining fire.

My old friend and adviser, whose presence I had felt more than seen the last few days, now forsook me altogether. But I was not alone. By some process my arms, legs, and stomach were transformed into so many traveling companions. Often for hours I would plod along conversing with these imaginary friends. Each had his peculiar wants that he expected me to supply. The stomach was importunate in his demand for a change of diet—and complained incessantly of the roots I fed him.

The others would generally concur with him in these fancied altercations. The legs implored me for rest, and the arms complained that I gave them too much to do. Troublesome as they were, it was a pleasure to realize their presence. I worked for them, too, with light good will, doing many things for their seeming comfort which, had I felt myself alone, would have remained undone. They appeared to be perfectly helpless of themselves and would do nothing for me or for each other.

One day I came to a small stream issuing from a spring of mild temperature on the hillside, swarming with minnows. I caught some with my hands and ate them raw. To my taste they were delicious. But the stomach refused them, accused me of attempting to poison him, and would not be reconciled until I had emptied my pouch of the few fish I had put there for future use. Those that I ate made me very sick. Had I glutted my appetite with them as I intended, I should doubtless have died in excruciating torment.

As I struggled along, my thoughts would revert to the single being on whom my holiest affections centered—my daughter. What a tie was that to bind me to life! Oh! could I be restored to her for a single hour, long enough for parting counsel and blessing, it would be joy unspeakable! Long hours of painful travel were relieved of physical suffering by this absorbing agony of the mind, which, when from my present standpoint I contrast it with the personal calamities of my exile, swells into mountains.

To return from this digression, at many of the streams on my route I spent hours in endeavoring to catch trout, with a hook fashioned from the rim of my broken spectacles, but in no instance with success. The tackle was defective.

At Tower Falls I spent the first half of a day in capturing a grasshopper, and the remainder in a fruitless effort to catch a mess of trout. In the agony of disappointment, I resolved to fish no more.

Soon after leaving Tower Falls, I entered the open country. Pine forests and windfalls were changed for sagebrush and desolation, with occasional tracts of stinted verdure. My first camp on this part of the route, for the convenience of getting wood, was made near the summit of a range of towering foothills.

Towards morning a storm of wind and snow nearly extinguished my fire. The storm was still raging when I arose, and the ground white with snow. I was perfectly bewildered, and had lost my course of travel. No visible object, seen through the almost blinding storm, reassured me, and there was no alternative but to find the river and take my direction from its current.

Fortunately, after a few hours of stumbling and scrambling among rocks and over crests, I came to the precipitous side of the canyon through which it ran, and with much labor, both of hands and feet, descended it to the margin. I drank copiously of its pure waters, and sat beside it for a long time, waiting for the storm to abate, so that I could procure fire.

The day wore on, without any prospect of a termination to the storm. Chilled through, my tattered clothing saturated, I saw before me a night of horrors unless I returned to my fire. The scramble up the side of the rocky canyon, in many places nearly perpendicular, was the hardest work of my journey. Often while clinging to the jutting rocks with hands and feet, to reach a shelving projection, my grasp would unclose and I would slide many feet down the sharp declivity.

It was night when, sore from the bruises I had received, I reached my fire. The storm, still raging, had nearly extinguished it. I found a few embers in the ashes, and with much difficulty kindled a flame. Here, on this bleak mountainside, as well as I now remember, I must have passed two nights beside the fire, in the storm.

Many times during each night I crawled to the little clump of trees to gather wood, and brush, and the broken limbs of fallen treetops. All the sleep I obtained was snatched from the intervals that divided these labors. I was so harassed with frightful dreams as to afford little rest.

I remember, before I left this camp, stripping up my sleeves to look at my shrunken arms. Flesh and blood had apparently left them. The skin clung to the bones like wet parchment. A child's hand could have clasped them from wrist to shoulder. "Yet," thought I, "it is death to remain; I cannot perish in this wilderness."

My supply of thistle roots was running low, and there were yet several days of heavy mountain travel between me and Bottler's Ranch. With the most careful economy, it could last but two or three days longer. I saw the necessity of placing myself and imaginary companions upon allowance. The conflict which ensued with the stomach, when I announced this resolution, required great firmness to carry through. I tried wheedling and coaxing and promising; failing in these, I threatened to part company with a comrade so unreasonable, and he made no further complaint.

Two or three days before I was found, I fell from exhaustion into the sagebrush. Unbuckling my belt, as was my custom, I soon fell asleep. I have no idea of the time I slept, but upon awaking I fastened my belt, scrambled to my feet, and pursued my journey.

As night drew on I selected a camping place, gathered wood into a heap, and felt for my lens to procure fire. It was gone. The floodgates of misery seemed now to be opened, and it rushed in living tide upon my soul. With the rapidity of lightning, I ran over every event of my life. Thoughts doubled and trebled upon me, until I saw, as if in vision, the entire past of my existence. It was all before me, as if painted with a sunbeam, and all seemingly faded like the phantoms of a vivid dream.

As calmness returned, reason resumed her empire. Fortunately, the weather was comfortable. I summoned all the powers of my memory, thought over every foot of the day's travel, and concluded that the glass must have become detached from my belt while sleeping. Five long miles over the hills must be retraced to regain it. There was no alternative, and before daylight I had staggered over half the distance. I found the lens on the spot where I had slept. No incident of my journey brought with it more of joy and relief.

Returning to the camp of the previous night, I lighted the pile I had prepared and lay down for a night of rest. It was very cold, and towards morning snowing commenced. With difficulty I kept the fire alive. Sleep was impossible.

When daylight came, I was impressed with the idea that I must go on despite the storm. In the afternoon the storm abated and the sun shone at intervals. Coming to a small clump of trees, I set to work to prepare a camp. I laid the brand down to pick up a few dry sticks with which to feed it, until I could collect wood for a campfire. In the few minutes thus employed it expired. I sought to revive it, but every spark was gone.

Clouds obscured the sun, now near the horizon, and the prospect of another night of exposure without fire became fearfully imminent. I sat down with my lens and the last remaining piece of touchwood I possessed to catch a gleam of sunshine, feeling that my life depended on it. In a few moments the cloud passed, and with trembling hands I presented the little disk to the face of the glowing luminary.

Quivering with excitement lest a sudden cloud should interpose, a moment passed before I could hold the lens steadily enough to concentrate a burning focus. At length it came. The little thread of smoke curled gracefully upwards from the Heaven-lighted spark, which, a few moments afterwards, diffused with warmth and comfort my desolate lodgings.

I resumed my journey the next morning, with the belief that I should make no more fires with my lens. I must save a brand, or perish. The day was raw and gusty; an east wind, charged with storm, penetrated my nerves with irritating keenness. After walking a few miles the storm came on, and a coldness unlike any other I had ever felt seized me. It entered all my bones. I attempted to build a fire, but could not make it burn.

A solemn conviction that death was near overwhelmed me with terror. Amid all this tumult of the mind, I felt that I had done all that man could do. I knew that in two or three days more I could effect my deliverance. I derived no little satisfaction from the thought that, as I was now in the broad trail, my remains would be found, and my friends relieved of doubt as to my fate.

Once only the thought flashed across my mind that I should be saved, and I seemed to hear a whispered command to "Struggle on." Groping along the side of a hill, I became suddenly sensible of a sharp reflection, as of burnished steel. Looking up, through half-closed eyes, two rough but kindly faces met my gaze.

"Are you Mr. Everts?"

"Yes. All that is left of him."

"We have come for you."

"Who sent you?"

"Judge Lawrence and other friends."

"God bless him, and them, and you! I am saved!" With these words I fell forward into the arms of my preservers, in a state of unconsciousness. I was saved. On the very brink of the river which divides the known from the unknown, strong arms snatched me from the final plunge, and kind ministrations wooed me back to life.

Baronet and Prichette, my two preservers, soon restored me to consciousness and made a camp upon the spot. One went to Fort Ellis, a distance of seventy miles, to return with remedies to restore digestion and an ambulance to convey me to that post. The other sat by my side, and with all the care, sympathy, and solicitude of a brother, he ministered to my frequent necessities.

In two days I was sufficiently recovered in strength to be moved twenty miles down the trail to the cabin of some miners who were prospecting in that vicinity. From these men I received every possible attention which their humane and generous natures could devise. A good bed was provided, game was killed to make broth, and the best stores of their larder placed at my command. For four days, at a time when every day's labor was invaluable in their pursuit, they abandoned their work to aid in my restoration. Owing to the protracted inaction of the system, and the long period which must transpire before Prichette's return with remedies, my friends had serious doubts of my recovery.

The night after my arrival at the cabin, while suffering the most excruciating agony, and thinking that I had only been saved to die among friends, a loud knock was heard at the cabin door. An old man in mountain costume entered— a hunter, whose life was spent among the mountains. He was on his way to find a brother. He listened to the story of my sufferings, and tears rapidly coursed each other down his rough, weather-beaten face. But when he was told of my present necessity, brightening in a moment, he exclaimed:

"Why, Lord bless you, if that is all, I have the very remedy you need. In two hours' time all shall be well with you."

He left the cabin, returning in a moment with a sack filled with the fat of a bear that he had killed a few hours before. From this he rendered out a pint measure of oil. I drank the whole of it. It proved to be the needed remedy, and the next day, freed from pain, with appetite and digestion reestablished, I felt that only good food and plenty of it were necessary for an early recovery.

In a day or two I took leave of my kind friends, with a feeling of regret at parting, and of gratitude for their kindness as enduring as life. Meeting the carriage along the way, I proceeded to Bozeman, where I remained among old friends, who gave me every attention until my health was sufficiently restored to allow me to return to my home at Helena.

HENRY "BIRD" CALFEE

———ᗰᗰ———

*T*he return of the Washburn Expedition in 1870 caused an
enormous stir in Montana. Territorial newspapers immediately published short accounts of the trip, and more detailed
articles came out over the next few weeks. These accounts
confirmed rumors that had circulated for decades and moti-
vated dozens of Montanans to see the upper Yellowstone for
themselves. Among them were a young painter, Henry "Bird"
Calfee, and his friend Macon Josey.

They set out as soon as the snow melted in the spring of
1872. They were traveling at a leisurely pace and having a
good time until Josey fell into a geyser. Then Calfee had to
figure out a way to move his scalded friend, find food when
supplies ran low, and elude horse thieves they encountered
on their way home.

Calfee's account of the trip was found in a clipping from
an unidentified newspaper at the Pioneer Museum in Bozeman, Montana. It was published about 1896.

Calfee continued to visit the park for several years and
became one of the first photographers to set up a commercial
business there selling stereopticon views of the sights. He also
took the lantern views that W. W. Wylie used for his national
lecture tour extolling the park in 1881–1882. Wylie also used
woodcuts based on Calfee's photographs to illustrate his 1882
Yellowstone guidebook.

Although Calfee doesn't mention photography in this memoir of his 1871 trip (apparently he took up photography later), he eventually took nearly three hundred pictures in Yellowstone.

In his account Calfee says the trip took place in 1871, but that apparently is in error. Calfee says the travelers visited Yankee Jim's cabin in the canyon that bears his name, but Jim didn't arrive there until 1872. Also, the horse thieves that Calfee and Josey encountered were the notorious Harlow gang, which had been stealing horses for several months. Based on information provided by Calfee and Josey, Bozeman sheriff J. C. Guy formed a posse that tracked down the Harlow gang and engaged them in a gun battle killing three of the outlaws. Newspaper accounts place this incident in 1872.

SAVING A SCALDED MAN—1871

From Henry Calfee's memoir

Early in the spring of 1870, I came to Montana in company with Mr. Macon Josey and located in Bozeman. I engaged in the painting business and my companion in shoemaking.

During the summer fabulous reports came in from the upper Yellowstone region of the existence of astounding wonders. And great was excitement in the then quiet little village of Bozeman, especially among the late arrivals. Josey and I were not long in making up our minds to go and see for ourselves the world's most wonderful phenomena. The season then being too far advanced to make an extended trip, we determined on an early start the following spring.

During the winter and early spring we got everything in readiness for a summer's exploration. As soon as the weather would permit, we started on our journey, armed to the teeth for Indians, buffalo and bear, in which the country at that time abounded, little dreaming of the perils and hardships that were laying in store for us before we would reach civilization again. The immense amount of snow that had fallen during the winter greatly hindered our progress. We were ten days in reaching Yankee Jim's abode in the second canyon of the Yellowstone. We stopped with him a few days, trouting and shooting mountain sheep, which were abundant in those days. We listened attentively to his sheep and bear stories, and he passed us through his portals into Wonderland free of charge.

Early travelers to Yellowstone Park carried few supplies and planned to supplement their meager larders with the plentiful game like these hunters at Yellowstone Lake.
National Park Service photo by F. J. Haines, 1883

A few days later we reached Mammoth Hot Springs, the crowning beauty of Wonderland. We lingered around these marvelous formations for two weeks and then journeyed on up the Yellowstone. Our next object of interest was Tower Falls. In this vicinity we stopped four or five days, then began the ascent of Mount Washburn, which we attained with great difficulty after three days' wallowing through mud, snow, and ice. We were too early in the season for the scenic splendor visible from its summit later in the season, as it was one vast expanse of snow and dark forests of pine, and being nearly snow blind we were in no mood to go into ecstasy over it. With equal difficulty we made the summit and reached the Great Falls and Grand Canyon.

After ten days' camping in this vicinity of indescribable grandeur we reluctantly started for the Sulphur Mountain and Mud Volcano, which was at that time in eruption every six hours. Viewing these phenomenal wonders for a day or two, we went on to the Yellowstone Lake. We camped four or five days, taking it leisurely in order that the snow might have time to disappear on the divide between the lake and geyser country, which was our next objective point. After an unsuccessful attempt to cross direct from the lake to the geysers we were obliged to return to the Mud Volcano.

By this time we were almost out of provisions, and entirely out of store victuals. Bread and meat, straight without salt, was our bill of fare. Meat, however, was in abundance. It consisted of buffalo, moose, elk, bear, wolverine, black and white tail deer, antelope, mountain sheep, goat or ibex, fox, coyote, badger, otter, beaver, mink, marten, sable, rabbit, porcupine, rock-dog, squirrel, skunk, grouse, goose, duck, crane, owl, raven, blackbird, blue-jay, curlew, sage, prairie chicken, and trout, with which the upper Yellowstone and lake abounded. This bill seems elaborate, but all could be gotten within five miles of our camp and in a very short time. The little prairie on which we were camped was the only bare ground for many miles around and the game seemed to have flocked to it from every direction.

From the Mud Volcano we moved our camp directly across the prairie to Alum Geyser. It was a little insignificant thing, although we considered it wonderful, as it was the first natural clear fluid projector we had seen. Here we killed an elk and a buffalo and fire-dried quite a quantity of meat; enough we thought to do us home as we thought it would be better eating without salt than fresh meat.

With considerable difficulty we crossed the Madison Range and in a few days we were in the midst of the Fire Dominion, viewing many scenes that had probably never before been witnessed by the human eye. Here in this realm of beauty, grandeur, and magnificence our joy knew no bounds. Could anyone accustomed to the scenes have seen our actions they would have taken us for lunatics. All our previous troubles and hardships and tedious traveling through pathless forests and over precipitous mountains, scrambling over down timber through slush, mud, and snow, were forgotten in the presence of such marvelous wonders. Amid this vast assemblage of transporting beauty and novelty, our privations did not concern it in the least. Grub or no grub, we soon made up our minds to stay ten days, at least. It was here, among these gorgeous scenes of fabulous grandeur, that I conceived the idea of getting up my Wonderland entertainment, which I succeeded in doing a few years later.

On the morning of the third day we were suddenly brought to realize that the pleasures of our romantic journey were at an end, and that our perils and hardships had just commenced. While out exploring and gathering treasured specimens on a tributary of the Firehole River we scared a deer out of a small bunch of timber, which, in its frightened condition attempted to bound over a large open geyser that was in its line of retreat. Failing to land with its hind feet on the farther edge of the formation, it fell backwards into the boiling caldron. We hastened to its rescue and attempted to raise it out by thrusting a long pole under its belly. The formation gave way with us, my companion going down with the deer into the horrible seething pool. I narrowly escaped by falling backward into the solid form formation.

I assisted my companion as quickly as possible, but in one half minute he was scalded from his waist down. He was so badly scalded that when I pulled off his boots and socks the flesh rolled off with them. I managed to get him back to camp and put what little remaining flour we had on his raw and bleeding burns.

I began immediately making preparations for an early start the next morning for the settlement on the Madison River below. I expected to reach them in two days, but so slow was our progress that we were scarcely out of sight of the Lower Geyser Basin at the end of that time. I hastily constructed a travois after the Indian style, in which Josey could ride; I carefully packed our specimens in bark and grass for their safe transit.

I then went up to the Old Faithful Geyser to whom we had delivered our washing the morning before starting out. I found it all nicely washed and lying on his pearly pavement ready for delivery. Our linen and cotton garments, which had been stiff and black with dirt lay there as white as the driven snow and our woolen clothes were as clean as could be. But oh my, imagine them in that mammoth unpatented washing machine boiling for one solid hour and then imagine my one hundred and sixty-five pound carcass inside of a suit of underwear scarcely large enough for a ten-year-old boy. I said to Old Faithful, you are a mighty good laundryman but you will not do up my flannels anymore. I went back to camp regretting that we couldn't stay in his vicinity long enough to patronize him again.

Night came on and with it a beautiful clear sky and full moon, I took my gun and went out viewing the amazing wonders until a late hour. Up to this time it is safe to say that there was never two persons who had a more romantic and enjoyable time than Josey and I. It was one continual round of pleasure.

Early next morning I got up and got breakfast, which was not a very laborious job as it consisted of elk, straight. I saddled and packed up, got Josey into his travois and started down the river, reluctantly leaving behind us the world's most marvelous wonders, many of which were yet to be won by human eye, and I here resolved to return as soon as circumstances would permit.

We were all day getting to the Lower Geyser Basin, all of ten miles. We camped near the Fountain Geyser, and as we were leaving next morning it began spouting. Josey asked me to lead his horse around where he could have a good view of the eruption that continued at least a half hour. Josey declared he could have lain there all day, suffering as he was, and watch such displays of natural magnificence and grandeur. I doubt whether distress and pain could relieve him of all desire for such displays of natural beauty. We bade goodbye to the Fountain, started on our journey.

When I began this letter, it was not my intention to mention any bear stories, which were nearly every-day occurrences, but in one instance it came so near resulting in a repetition of the lamentable accident two days previous that I will relate it.

As we were leaving the geysers I saw a large bear about a mile ahead of us. I said to myself, "Old fellow, if you stay there until I get up in shouting distance, I'll fix you." We traveled along slowly until we got within about 150 yards of it. By this time it looked very large. I stopped and got off my horse.

As Josey was riding on his back with his head forward, he could not see what was going on in front. He asked what was the matter, and I told him there was a bear in front and I was going to turn his toes up.

He said to me: "You had better go on and let the bear alone. You are liable to get eaten up yet by some of your foolishness, besides you will scare the horses and I am liable to get hurt in this damned arrangement. Go on and let the bear go to hell."

He evidently did not have much faith in my tackling the bear alone. But I paid no attention to what he said. I began to approach the bear and accidentally stumbled over a root and he discovered me. He did not seem frightened or in any way concerned at my presence except he grunted a little, which I mistook for a growl a minute or two later.

I walked up within seventy-five yards of the bear and would have gone closer had not the creek been in the way.

A minute later this proved to be a life preserver for me. I raised my rifle and fired, and down went the bruin to the ground with a terrible growl. It was up again and to my great surprise there was at her side a large cub. She began growling, biting and knocking the cub, and it began bellowing unmercifully. I put another cartridge in my gun as quick as possible and fired. By this time all was in confusion. The horses were snorting and running. Josey was yelling "whoa, whoa" at the top of his voice and "for Lord sake, catch my horse." But I had no time to catch horses then.

The maddened beast left her cub, and with the most unearthly growl I ever heard, the infuriated monster made direct for me. By the time I got my gun loaded that vicious terror was lunging into the creek over fifty feet from me. I fired again. While putting another cartridge in my gun, I looked around and saw that both Josey and the horse were in imminent danger. I almost flew to their rescue. One second longer and they would have been in a seemingly bottomless cauldron of boiling water. The horse was running around and around with his head pulled back against the saddle skirt by a rope which I had tied into the bridle bit and passed back to Josey in case he should want to stop at any time. The horse could not see where he was going, and Josey was lying in his "man killer," as he called it, pulling on the rope with all his might. I retreated with them to a safe distance from both bear and geyser and there stood almost breathless and spellbound while Josey gave me one of the most severe reprimandings I ever received in my life. The profanity he used would have made a cannibal shudder.

When I came to myself and realized what had happened, I looked around to see Old Bolly with the packsaddle under his belly and still bucking. I helped Josey out of the travois and sat him up against a tree and told him he could, in case of necessity, climb, instead of running. He said, "What! Are you going tackle that infernal bear again?"

"No," I said, "not unless she tackles me."

He then gave me a sarcastic look and said, "You have played hell haven't you?"

"No," said I, "but you came so near going there a little while ago that my heart hasn't quit beating yet."

"Yes," he said, "it was that old bear that caused your heart to beat, and if you tackle another bear on this trip, I hope you will be eaten up."

I picked up my rifle and started after the other horses when Josey said to me, "Leave that gun here with me."

"No sir," said I, "if that bear eats anyone up, it had better be a half dead man than a live one." That gave rise to another outburst of profanity.

I went on and caught the other horses and brought them back, I then began gathering up the wreck or what I could find of it. Our specimens, petrified snakes, fish, grasshoppers, bugs, one petrified bird, and many other things, all natural as life, and the very choice of this national heritage of wonders, lay scattered and smashed to smithereens. As I looked on the wreck, I swore eternal vengeance against the bear race, but I will say right here that I never went around hunting them for the express purpose of revenge.

I packed up and got everything in readiness to move on. I then told Josey I was going back to take a look at the bear before starting and that I was quite sure she was lying in the water dead.

He began at once pleading with me not to go, he argued with me that she was lying there in the water wounded and for Heaven's sake not to molest her and get her riled up again, for he was in no condition to stand any more frights.

I argued with him, but gave way to his earnest pleadings, although I was convinced the bear was dead. I would have given the best packhorse we had to have known for an absolute certainty whether she was in her watery grave or lying there bathing her wounds. It would have been a source of great pleasure to me in after years. When steaming up and down the lower Missouri, my mind would sometimes wander to its very source in the Wonderland. Looking down, into its placid depths I would wonder if there was not some of its waters that had passed over the decaying bones of that formidable green-eyed monster of the Rocky Mountains.

We journeyed along until camping time without any more mishaps. By this time Josey had begun to get very sore and quite unwell, and it was only with my utmost exertions that I could do everything to please him.

We left camp the next morning with the faint hope of reaching the settlements next day, but in a very short time it became evident to me that our troubles had just begun, and traveling was only another name for scrambling, winding, crawling, and climbing.

In attempting to follow game trails we were often snared into dangerous places. At one place I followed a nice open trail into a canyon and passed over some very dangerous places and thought each one was the last. Presently our trail ran out and we were then on the side of the canyon where it was impossible for a horse to turn around. It was all slide rock, and every step our horses made would move more tons of it. It was necessary to keep moving in order to keep from being precipitated into the river hundreds of feet below.

I helloed to Josey to stop. He was in the rear of the pack-horses, but he had gotten too far into the shale rock to stop, and it was impossible for his horse to turn around with the long poles of the travois. The horses themselves seemed to realize the danger they were in and began to scramble for themselves to the top of the canyon, which all luckily reached, breathless and excited as they looked back at the moving earth and rock they had just passed over. It was a narrow escape, and it made my blood curdle as I gazed upon it and into the roaring torrent a thousand feet below.

Poor Josey, lying there in his man-killer with a death grip still on the poles, he had not realized to the fullest extent the dangers he had gone through. I expected another reprimanding, but not until I took him out of his travois in order to rearrange it, did he say a word. He crawled to the brink of that terrible abyss and looked over into it where the rock was still rolling down. Then he said: "Bird, whatever possessed you to take me into such a place as that? I see you are determined to kill me yet. It would have been far preferable if you had left me in the geyser than to have tortured me in this manner. There is no use talking, I will never ride another foot in that arrangement. You needn't bother any longer fixing it. I'd as well take a gun and blow my head off and be done with it. I will never travel another step unless I can see where you are taking me."

I told him I had been thinking all day of abandoning the travois because it was not a practical arrangement for the rough pathless country. If he would ride in it until I found a place to camp, I would stop and contrive something in which he could ride and see where he was going. And I said I would avoid all dangerous-looking places.

We soon found a nice camping place on a little creek that I could almost step across. As I had to use considerable water on Josey's account, I stretched the tent as close to the stream as possible. During the night it began to rain, and in two hours the little creek was a roaring torrent. I barely had time to take Josey to a safe place when our tent was flooded and a great many things went down the stream. We laid over the next day and dried out. The creek flowed through a marshy flat below, where I recovered most of our things. It was by accident I found our sack of buffalo meat almost covered over in the mud.

The substitute for the travois was a stretcher with a horse at each end of it. In open country it was dandy; but like the travois, it would not work in the timber and we had to abandon it, too. I then rigged up an arrangement by which he could sit on the horse with his legs crossed over the horse's neck, as it was almost death to let his legs hang down. And in this manner he rode to the end of the journey.

To add to our trouble and Josey's suffering came the abominable flies and mosquitoes. At times they were almost unendurable. It seemed as if they had driven every living thing in the valley to the icy heights and had congregated to devour us and our horses.

On the morning of the fifth day out from the geyser basin, we imagined we could see smoke rising from the settlements and were buoyed up by the thoughts of getting out of the wilderness. Josey insisted on giving directions as to the course to travel. We finally struck a beautiful game trail almost as wide as a wagon road. It did not run exactly in the direction I wanted to go; but Josey insisted on traveling on it as long as it would run anywhere near the direction we wanted to go.

I followed it until it led off into a growth of young pine when I refused to go any farther. Josey swore he intended following the trail as long as it lasted. I told him there was down timber in that forest as thick as the hair on a dog's back and for him not to attempt to go through it. I turned to the left, believing he would follow me, but he was bent on traveling the trail and down the hill he went, with the pack-horses following him, and soon disappeared in the brush.

I spurred up my horse and rode at good speed around to where I could plainly see him bobbing up and down as his horse went over logs down the hill. His trail ran out, or, in other words, scattered as mine did in the canyon. It was impossible for him to get back up the hill. He turned in the direction I had gone as his horse attempted to lunge over a high log.

I got off and hitched my horse and helloed to him and asked if he was coming. I waited quite a while and yelled out to him to come on. I then went closer and repeated the same question. I was then in a humor to tantalize him a little so I told him to come on if he was going to and if not to say so, and I would go on. He then hallowed and told me he was compelled to ask my assistance; that he had gotten into a trap and could not possibly get out alone.

I went to him and found him in the meshes of the worst timber net I had ever seen. I said nothing but took the ax and began chopping a way for Josey to crawl out. I then got him up on my back and carried him to where I had left my horse and left him to fight flies and mosquitoes until I could extricate the horses.

I went back and chopped the log that Josey's horse was hanging over. I made an attempt to get them back the way they had come in, but it was no go. I then tried to drive them out. They seemed to realize their imprisoned condition and would not make any exertion to help themselves. I pulled their packs and saddles off and turned them loose, and then attempted to drive them.

I took the infernal old ax that had not seen a grindstone in three months, and chopped several logs to give them a start, believing that once started they would keep going; but they soon stopped. It was then for the first time my temper got the entire control of my better judgment. It is not necessary for me to mention my thoughts and expressions and it is only those who have traveled pathless mountains that can imagine or form any adequate idea of them or the difficulties in such places. I cut a green pine switch, or rather pole, and went at them, and in less than three minutes I had all of them hanging across logs. Old Bolly was entirely off the earth.

The old ax was my only resort. I grabbed it and went at it letting Old Bolly out first. I finally got them all on the ground again and I wondered if I would have to carry them out as I did in Josey's case. After three hours continuous wielding that old meat ax, I succeeded in laying enough of that forest on the ground to get the horses out.

By this time I was about famished for water. I made one trip back to where I had unpacked after a load and to get coffee and to get Josey a little water to quench his thirst too. I got on my horse and started in the direction we could plainly hear water roaring which was about half a mile away. When I reached the roaring, I drank as long as

I could of the ice-cold water. I then stepped onto the same log as I had done before to refill the coffee pot, and down I went into the foaming torrent that carried me at a fearful rate, tossing and slamming me as though I was a wooden man, and wrapped me around a boulder one hundred yards below, almost drowned. When I came to myself I did not know hardly what had happened. And strange to say I still had a firm grip on that old black coffee pot until I scrambled out and sat down on the rocks. I then realized what a narrow escape I had made from a watery grave. I found my hat lodged in a drift which I had certainly passed under. Holding the coffee pot saved my life. If hadn't been holding it, I would undoubtedly have caught onto something under the drift and would have drowned.

I got on my horse and went back to where I had left Josey and handed him the pot of water. He exclaimed, "Great Heavens, man, you have been sweating terribly."

"I should say so," said I, "and had it not been for a big boulder that rolled out of that yawning canyon yonder, I would now have been passing through the settlements on the Madison River."

I then told him what a narrow escape I had from drowning, and the big tears began to roll down his cheeks.

After two hours hard work carrying out the packs and saddles and packing up again, we were ready to continue our journey, and as it was late in the afternoon we intended to camp as soon as we found a suitable place. We crossed over the creek where I came so near to losing my life. I pointed out the boulder against which I had been lodged, and it seemed more miraculous that I escaped because the water was so swift that the horses could hardly stand in it.

We had traveled but a short distance when we noticed what appeared to be an open country just ahead of us. As we watched that charming spot, Josey discovered a house in the distance. As he was pointing it out, I plainly saw a large herd of stock.

"Thank Heavens," exclaimed Josey, "the settlements at last. Hurry up and we'll have the pleasure of sleeping under one more dirt roof before we die."

With renewed energy we jogged along, passing several good camping places, but as the sun was fast setting it soon became evident that we would have to camp one more night in the wilderness. We were not long in selecting a nice spot and arranging things as comfortable as possible. After eating our scanty morsel of meat we soon retired for the night, tired and worn out, and the doings of that eventful day were soon forgotten.

Cheered by that picturesque scene of human abode, we arose with the sun next morning to gaze out on the long-sought homes of the pioneers of the Madison. But instead of that transformation scene rose a vision of low foothills, scarred with ravines, craggy cliffs, and gorges. Not until then did we realize that we had been deceived and made victims of a ghostly mirage of some other valley, perhaps sixty or seventy miles away.

With this disappointment Josey began to get despondent at times and very irritable at others. He would quarrel at his horse and threaten to kill him in all imaginable ways. I was obliged to help him off his horse every half hour to rest during the entire trip. He began to want to rest all the time. Conscious of the need of food and proper attention for him gave me a great uneasiness and anxiety. I was compelled to act very determined with him at all times, so much so that he would threaten me with all kinds of violence. He would tell me that I was an idiot and that it only required a trip in the mountains to find a man out. This assertion is correct for what is in a man will come out in the mountains if nowhere else.

Most of our meat was spoiled by the flood and flies so we were obliged to throw it away. We ate the remainder that morning for our breakfast and packed up. With lingering hopes we journeyed on, watching for an opportunity to shoot something to eat. None came on and not a living thing had been seen. The mosquitoes had driven everything into the high mountains. We moved near a cliff in which there was a rock dog, which at our presence kept up a continual barking.

I said, "Old fellow, you have stood off the mosquitoes nobly and if you will just keep up that racket until I get done unpacking, I'll go you a round." I asked Josey if he thought he could go dog meat. He said anything was preferable to that damn old sandy buffalo meat he had been eating. I took my gun, a 50-caliber Sharps rifle, and went for the dog. I tried in every way to get an opportunity to shoot his head off, but all in vain. He was in his hole and his head was in line with his body. I then thought I would just graze one side of his head and body.

I fired and killed him, but the ball took the meat off and left me only the skin. I went and got it and took it down to Josey and told him there was the skin, but the dog had gone back in his hole. By that time our usual camp pests (mountain jay birds) began to congregate and I began the difficult task of braining jay birds with 50-caliber balls that would in passing through an elk take meat enough for a coyote's feast. I managed to get four or five birds or parts of birds. I cleaned and boiled them for Josey. He insisted on me helping him eat them but I told him no, that it would do me more good to see him eat and if I did not succeed in getting meat that afternoon that we would try one of Old Bolly's hind quarters.

After a good rest we jogged along. The country looked a little more favorable both for game and habitation. We had not gone far when I discovered something ahead of us in the brush, shaking it as though it intended scaring all the mosquitoes out of the country. I dismounted as quickly as possible and began to approach the brush with the calculation of tackling whatever it might be, even if it was the devil himself.

When Josey noticed my activities and saw the shaking of the brush, he called to me and asked what it was. I motioned him to keep quiet. By this time he had gotten a glimpse of it and thought it was a large bear. He then yelled at the top of his voice at me. "Don't shoot, hold on, help me off my horse and give me my gun." His noise frightened my prey and away it went before I had an opportunity to see it. I did not get sight of it until it was out of shooting distance. Then I saw it was an enormous bull moose. I could have walked within ten steps of him and blown the very liver out of him before he could have known there was a man within ten miles, had Josey kept his infernal mouth shut.

Mad, mad is no name for it. It makes me mad to this day when I think of it. I had not talked saucy to Josey since his accident at the geyser. Not a bite to eat and for him to yell, "Don't shoot." I tell you that did rile the bile in me. I went back and asked him what under heaven tempted him to bellow in that manner. I told him I was tempted to take him off that horse and wear the earth with him, and if he ever opened that infernal mouth of his again when I wanted to shoot, I would wipe him from the face of the earth.

We went along for about an hour and my clothes began to fit me a little better. I stopped and helped Josey off his horse and gave him a drink of water. As he took the cup from his feverish lips, he said it tasted good. "Yes," I said, "but eight or ten pounds of that old moose would have tasted a darn sight better."

I told him under the present circumstances we had better camp there and I would go out and rustle something to eat. If there was anything in the country to be had, I was going to have it. I intended to fill up my craw that night if I had to take a leg off Old Bolly to do it. I arranged camp and started off. Josey asked me not to stay out too late and told me I had better give him a little more water before I went away. While I was dipping water from the little stream I saw a number of small fish and it occurred to me that where there were many small ones there might be some larger ones.

I took the shovel and in a few minutes had the water turned out of the channel. I went above two hundred yards and cut a green pine bough and went down the little stream, slapping and pounding and scaring everything before me. When I came to the little dam, imagine my surprise, for the whole hillside seemed to be alive with fish flipping and floundering in all directions. Eureka—a fish feast, grub in abundance. Old Bolly has an extension of time in which to prepare himself more toothsome purposes. Mr. Moose is not wanted now.

The remainder of the day I put in cleaning and boiling fish, occasionally I would get far enough ahead with my job to sit down and assist Josey in eating the remainder of a kettleful. I don't mean to insinuate that Josey was a big fish eater, but I will say that it was a gallon and a half camp kettle that I was cooking them in and you must not suppose that I would fool away any time in cooking it half full at a time. I will also say that Josey was built just right for eating fish and if he would have only practiced I would have wagered all my capital on him getting himself on the outside of more fish than any other man in the Rocky Mountains. Had I an assistant I would have prevailed on him to have practiced as I could have gotten fish by the cartload.

Next we traveled along at a better speed. That afternoon we passed through the portals of that picturesque valley of the Madison and shook hands with a hardy pioneer, George Lyon, whose latch string hung outside of his dirt-covered mansion. As we rode up he stood in his yard with his ax in his hand silently gazing, full of wonder and amazement at the appearance of such a strange looking caravan.

Josey perched on his eminence with his head bundled up for protection from mosquitoes and with his legs crossed, resembled an Arab more than a geyser-crippled shoemaker. And I, with my geyser done-up clothes presented a spectacle which he had never seen before. And I have little doubt it would have attracted the attention of that celebrated showman, the late P. T. Barnum, could he have seen us.

We were welcomed, thrice welcomed, to the hospitalities of our host, and we were soon off our horses and at home. About the first thing I did was to introduce Josey to a cake of soap and a trough of water, after which there was little resemblance to the man who started out with me in the spring to explore the wonders of Yellowstone.

Our landlord soon spread out a bountiful supper, the best that a bachelor's culinary affords. After supper we sat around his open fireplace and narrated for the first time our perilous adventures. He listened attentively to all we said and pronounced us lucky to be alive. We retired at a late hour.

We stayed here two or three days until Josey felt sufficiently improved to continue our journey.

The hospitality of our host will never be forgotten. He gave us an instruction where to cross the Madison range and get into the West Gallatin River. We bade him goodbye with a God bless you and started on, expecting to meet our Bozeman friends in three days.

In crossing the range we lost the trail and began experiencing our same old difficulties. Traveling soon ceased and we began scrambling up the mountain. We finally reached the divide, and it seemed impossible to go any farther. At that point Josey suggested we go up higher in order that we might see our way out. We went up and up until we came out on a high open point. And there, spread before our vision a magnificent panorama of Gallatin Valley dotted with pioneer farms and hundreds of streams fluttering and glittering like ribbons of silver in the sunlight. Poor Josey, fatigued and with thoughts of the descent that he knew would not be accomplished without difficulties, did not get enthused over the scenic splendor. He only exclaimed, "My God, isn't that grand?"

Our descent was accomplished with great difficulty. Many places were hazardous for poor Josey. And his horse received many epithets coming down that mountain. As it was at his suggestion that we attained so great a height, he could not well use me for a target for his abuse. His horse, Old Panteo, as he called him, had the greatest burden of it. He declared he would never part with Old Panteo for any money because he intended killing him by degrees to get revenge.

When we got down on the Gallatin, we went into camp for the balance of the day and until noon the next day, when we started, calculating to camp on the West Gallatin River that night and the next night in Bozeman. We struck a good trail on a long ridge with a canyon on either side of us and were cheered by the thoughts of getting home and meeting friends. Little did we dream that there was yet another chapter to be added to our thrilling and blood-curdling adventures. We were to have a death sentence passed on us right in sight of our long-sought home.

While traveling down the ridge I noticed two men coming up the canyon on our right. I helloed back to Josey to cheer him up and told him come ahead because I had seen two men in the canyon below. I began to watch for an opportunity to go down into the canyon to meet the men, but there was none offered.

I rode down on the ridge until I came directly opposite the place where I last saw the men and stopped until Josey caught up. I pointed out the little bunch of brush to him and told him the men were in there. He said they were either elk or moose that I had seen and that there was no damn man on earth that would be traveling in such a place as that. I told him that they were men and acted as though they were hiding from us. Josey yelled at them but there was no answer. I said to him come on and let them go.

We went on down about one and a half miles and there in the same canyon we saw four more men and a large band of horses and mules. When the men discovered us, they all ran in the brush. Josey insisted on going down into their camp, but I told him to come on, that they were thieves. He still hesitated and I emphasized my next order with a mountain vocabulary and that brought him.

We traveled on down into a little valley and crossed the creek. I helped Josey off his horse and gave him a cup of water. Then we sat down in the shade to rest. We discussed the curious actions of the men we had passed. Josey was convinced they were prospectors. I told him I still was glad that I had acted as I did. At that time we dropped the subject, little thinking what we had just witnessed in the past two hours would be the cause of sending three souls unmercifully to eternity.

We began talking about our route, the advisability of going over the hill and so on, until the previous subject was entirely out of my mind. Suddenly something said to me in as plain words as I ever heard, "Get up and go." I realized that there was danger near at hand. I sprang to my horse and tightened the saddle on him. I said to Josey, "Let me help you on your horse," at the same time tightening his saddle.

When I helped him on he said, "Now give me my gun." I pulled his gun from the pack where it had been carried since his accident in the geyser, and gave it to him. Now he said, "Get on your horse and go, and go like hell too." As I had received commands from two sources I felt it was my duty to obey—and that quickly too.

About a mile in the direction I intended going was a small bunch of timber, which I thought would admirably suit our purpose. I reached the timber, making the fastest time I ever made on horseback. Josey was only a few rods behind me. The packhorses were not far in the distance, coming as though something had told them to get up and get, too. Here we took a rest.

I told Josey of the mysterious warning I had received and I realized that danger was near at hand. He said the moment he looked at me it had created a thrilling sensation that was equal to a warning. He really did not think we were out of danger yet because it was impossible for us to get to the settlements that night. He added that it would be an easy matter for the outlaws to waylay and shoot us from ambush—as they would undoubtedly do before they would allow us to escape.

I cleaned Josey's gun so it would fire all right and put him on his horse. I then told him I was going to take a direct course for the West Gallatin Canyon and would travel as fast as he liked. He told me to make good speed on level ground, as he could ride better than he imagined, and would let me know when to stop. By our brisk traveling we were able to reach the canyon about an hour before sundown, and to our great surprise met a party of prospectors from Bozeman.

We soon related our past few hours' experience. We told them of the mysterious commands we had received and the mysterious actions of the men we had seen and from whom we were supposed to be fleeing. We held a short consultation, and all concluded it was best to get back to the settlements that night if possible.

We unpacked to let our horses feed and rest. We got our supper and waited until dark, then packed up again, and before daylight next morning we were at old Uncle Kitt's across the West Gallatin River. There Josey got a team to carry him, and I managed to get home that day with the packs, thus ending one of my eventful journeys in the Rocky Mountains.

The news soon scattered that we had discovered the bandits, and a sheriff's posse was organized and I was induced to guide the party to where I had seen the mysterious actions of the men, and where I received my command to get up and go.

The party pursued them and I returned to Bozeman. Ten days afterward the sheriff returned with two prisoners and a quantity of stolen property. They shot three of the thieves dead, thus ending the Tom Harlow Bandits. The prisoners told about a council being held, in which it was decided that Josey and I should die.

THE EARL OF DUNRAVEN

—⟋m⟍—

Most early Yellowstone tourists came from the adjacent territories because getting to the park was too expensive for other people. But a few wealthy adventurers from distant places found the time and money to make the long trip. They had to travel to Utah on the new transcontinental railroad and then make an arduous stagecoach ride north through Idaho to Montana.

One such traveler was Windham Thomas Wyndam-Quin, the fourth Earl of Dunraven. Lord Dunraven, a fabulously wealthy Irish nobleman, hired several men to accompany him. One of them was Frederick Bottler, a rancher who settled in the Paradise Valley on the Yellowstone River in 1868. Bottler was familiar with Yellowstone's wonders and served as an outfitter, guide, and hunter for several early expeditions.

Dunraven, who had been a war correspondent for British newspapers, was an astute observer with a droll wit. In addition to his stories about watching geysers and hunting big game, he offers humorous advice on how to pack a mule, and tells about roasting fresh elk meat over a campfire.

He wrote several books about his travel adventures. The one excerpted here, The Great Divide, was his most popular.

THE GREAT DIVIDE—1874

From The Great Divide *by*
Windham Thomas Wyndam-Quin

On a lovely afternoon in the first week in August, we took the train from Salt Lake City, and arrived at Corinne, where we slept at a very comfortable little inn. We knew it would be our last night in bed for some time, so we made the most of the luxury. The following morning, at 6.30 a.m., we piled ourselves and traps into a lumbering, heavy, old-fashioned stagecoach, and, under the guidance of a whisky bottle and an exceedingly comical driver, started for Virginia City. Jehu was a very odd man and wore a very odd headdress, consisting of a chimney-pot hat elongated by some strange process into a cone, having the brim turned down and ventilated by large gashes cut in the sides. He was very garrulous, and, I grieve to add, profane. The coach was a strange vehicle, mostly composed of leather. It was decorated with decayed leather; the sides were leather curtains; the top was leather; it was hung upon leather straps, and thongs of the same material dangled from the roof.

The interior of the coach was occupied by three seats, the spaces between which we filled in with baggage, and over the comparatively level surface thus formed we were shot about like shuttles in a loom for four days and nights. The vehicle labored a great deal in the heavy roads, producing at first in most of us a feeling of seasickness, which gradually wore off. Friday, our first day out, was not pleasantly spent.

The abundant game attracted sport hunters from around the world before the army put a stop to the practice in 1883.
National Park Service Photo by W. H. Jackson, 1871

The sun was intensely powerful. The road, many inches deep in alkaline dust, traversed a level plain, following the course of Bear River; and there was nothing to break the dull monotony of the scene, except a few stunted artemisia and sage bushes, and very distant views of mountains. Clouds of the salt dust, agitated by the sultry breeze, covered our clothes, and filled our eyes, ears, noses, and mouths; dinner-time and tea-time were hailed with delight, and a little private eating and drinking was also indulged in to while away the tedious hours. There was no difficulty about eating, but to take a drink amidst the heavings and kickings of the carriage, without swallowing bottle and all, required considerable skill.

At length the long-wished-for shades of evening began to fall. The shadows of the mountains crept over the plain. The wind died away; the clouds of white powder settled down; and the delicious crisp coolness of a summer night at those high altitudes succeeded to the enervating suffocating heat of day and refreshed our irritated nerves. Rolling ourselves in blankets, we stretched out as well as we could upon the baggage and passed a very tolerable night. It was bright moonlight, and I lay awake for a long time watching the big jack-rabbits scudding over the plain, and admiring the jovial grinning countenance of the full moon; till, finally, in spite of the jolting, I fell into a sound sleep, broken, however, occasionally by the piercing Indian yells which the driver emitted to announce his approach to each station for changing horses.

Towards evening the plain narrowed into a valley, and the road became fearfully rough, littered with blocks of stone, and pitted with holes full of water. The depth of these pools not being properly laid down upon any chart, our driver was obliged to get off and sound them with his whip-handle, thereby delaying us very much.

During the night we crossed the mountains, and a little before sunrise awoke to find ourselves at a small change station close to the summit, and near to where the road branches off to Fort Hall.

On this particular Saturday morning the breaking of the day was very beautiful. There had been a slight frost. Not a single shred of vapor obscured the perfectly cloudless sky; not a breath of wind disturbed the marvelous transparency of the atmosphere. We stood on a very elevated plateau close to a solitary shanty. In the background were some half-dozen native lodges, from each of which rose in a straight line a thin blue thread of smoke. Crouched on the ground, his blanket drawn up over his mouth and nose, sat one Indian, and the gaunt figure of another was discernible stalking towards us in the rapidly decreasing gloom. The western constellations were still brightly shining, but the splendor of the morning star was waning before an intenser light.

Nothing is more extraordinary and wearisome than the levelness of the road. From Corinne to Virginia City you drive along a series of apparently perfectly flat plains, connected with each other by short canyons and valleys. Occasionally the road ascends, but by a very easy gradient. There are no precipices, no torrents, no avalanches, no glaciers— nothing grand, terrible, or dangerous. The idea that you are surmounting a portion of a great and important watershed, that you are crossing the backbone of the continent, and scaling a vast mountain range, appears preposterous.

As I do not consider it a wise thing to cook stories or varnish facts when one is sure to be found out, I must beg the reader to excuse my unfolding any hairbreadth escapes, and to suffer me to introduce him or her thus prosaically to Virginia City, where we arrived on Monday morning, in fair condition, but by no means according to sample, if one had been taken of us on leaving Deseret.

Virginia City. Good Lord! What a name for the place! We had looked forward to it during the journey as to a sort of haven of rest, a lap of luxury. There might have been laps, but there was no luxury. A street of straggling shanties, a bank, a blacksmith's shop, a few dry goods stores, and barrooms constitute the main attractions of the city. However, we soon became reconciled to our fate. We found the little inn very clean and comfortable. We dined on deer, antelope, and bear meat, a fact which raised hopes of hunting in our bosoms; and the people were exceedingly civil, kind, obliging, and anxious to assist strangers in any possible way, as, so far as my experience goes of America, and indeed of all countries, they invariably are as soon as you get off the regular lines of travel.

There was nothing to interest us in Virginia City, or in the neighborhood. The chances of good sport appeared on inquiry to be very doubtful, and so, as soon as we had rested ourselves, we decided, after a council of war, to go to Fort Ellis. The morning was cold and stormy, and the first snow of the year lay several inches deep on the slopes and summits of the two low divides over which the road passes.

The road, after pursuing a northeasterly direction for a few miles, crosses the Madison by a toll-bridge, and bends to the north along the margin of the stream. The Missouri, as I suppose all geography-taught folks are aware, heads in three principal streams, the Jefferson on the west, the Madison in the middle, and the Gallatin to the east. The Madison is, at the point of crossing, a fine, broad, rushing river, flowing with a current discolored by the washings of many placer mines, through a rich alluvial plain. In its shallow stream, warmed by the tributary waters of the Firehole River, the usual fluviatile vegetation flourishes with more than ordinary luxuriance, and fills the air with a clean, sea-weedy smell. Leaving the riverbed and turning again in an easterly direction, we crossed the low divide separating the Madison and Gallatin Valleys.

We reached the clear swift-flowing waters of the Gallatin about two in the afternoon, and, picking out a nice shady place, went into camp for a couple of hours. While some of us unhitched and unharnessed the horses, picketed them, and gave them their corn, others proceeded to the river and speedily returned with a dozen or so beautiful trout. A fire was soon lighted, and with fresh-broiled trout and some farinaceous [starchy] food, taken in a concentrated and liquid form out of a black bottle, we made a luncheon not to be despised, and then lay down in the cool shade to rest and wait till the hoses had finished their feed.

Oh! the comfort of lying flat on your back on the grass. I believe a man under such circumstances positively is nearly as happy as a cow in a clover field. It is sweet to do nothing; but we could not linger very long, for our destination, Fort Ellis, was at a distance unknown to us; so, hitching up the horses, we tucked ourselves into the buggy, crossed the Gallatin River, and pursued our way.

The valley of this river affords about the finest agricultural and pasture land in the territory. It is about forty miles in length from south to north, and varies in breadth from five to fifteen miles. It is watered by the Gallatin, the banks of which are very heavily bordered with poplars and bitter cottonwoods, and by several little tributaries, some rising on the eastern flanks of the Gallatin Range, and others towards the north, in a series of broken, detached, and unnamed mountains.

At the upper or south end of the valley stands the clean, all-alive, and wide-awake town of Bozeman; and three miles further on, almost in the jaws of Bozeman Pass, is Fort Ellis, the most important military post in the northwest. The term "fort" is in this, as in most other cases, a mere figure of speech. [Most trade and military establishments of the day were not fortified.] Fort Ellis consists of a large square, two sides of which are occupied by the soldiers' quarters, while the remaining side is devoted to the officers' houses. All along the inside of the square runs a wooden sidewalk, beside which a few unhappy trees are striving to grow; and the interior space, the centre of which is adorned with a tall flag-staff, is graveled, forming a commodious parade-ground; while the angles are flanked and protected by quaint old-fashioned–looking block houses, octagonal in shape, loop-holed, and begirt with a broad balcony, upon which sentries pace everlastingly up and down. Beyond the buildings forming the square are other soldiers' quarters, washerwomen's houses, stables, stores, billiard-room, blacksmith and saddler shops, and the like, the whole being surrounded by a sort of stockade fence; and furthest removed, on a breezy elevation, are the hospital buildings, and some large stores and magazines.

Strategically, the situation of Fort Ellis is well chosen, for it commands the valleys of the Yellowstone and of the three forks of the Missouri, in which is contained all the richest and best land in the territory—in fact, all that is really available for cultivation; and, in connection with Fort Shaw and Fort Benton, it commands the navigation on the Missouri, and the three principal passes which break through the mountains from one river system to the other. . . .

It was late in the afternoon when we arrived at Fort Ellis. With some difficulty we found our way to General Sweitzer's quarters, where, upon presenting our letters of introduction, we were most kindly received. By the time we had completed our ablutions, after which we stepped out on the "stoop," or veranda, to enjoy the cool breeze, the sun was nearly down. It was a most lovely evening. The atmosphere was "smoky," as it is termed in the West, and imparted a dim grandeur to the distant mountains, while the glowing valley lay basking in the sunlight; and far to the west the dark masses of the Madison Mountains bounded the horizon. Close by, the summits of Bridger's Peaks reared themselves distinct and clear, catching the full blaze of the setting sun; and to the north and east the blue cloudy heights of Crazy Woman Range swam and trembled in the haze. The air was perfectly still; the star-spangled banner hung motionless. Two or three cloud-islands, or rather reefs of clouds, lay in the clear blue sky, dazzling under the slant rays of the sun.

We had determined overnight to leave Fort Ellis early in the morning, so as to have plenty of time to reach Bottler's Ranch before dark. The trail emerges into a fine plain of about thirty miles in length and eight or ten in breadth. Near the head of this valley is Bottler's Ranch. We lay two days at Bottler's, hiring pack animals and manufacturing packing straps, hooks, and cinches; and we secured the services of Fred Bottler to act as our guide. Active, strong, willing and obliging, a keen hunter, always in good humor, capable of enduring great hardship, and a capital hand at making you comfortable in camp, I can confidently recommend him to anyone visiting these parts.

The following morning we made a start, and a most peculiar start it was. It was tedious to note the petty particulars of every day's progress. In place thereof, I will try to impart to the reader, once for all, some idea of the pleasures and miseries, the comforts and inconveniences, attendant upon packing.

Nothing is so abominably temper-trying as journeying with pack animals. Some of the beasts will not feed if they are picketed and, as it is essential that they eat well, you picket one or two only and turn loose the rest. You have a long way to go, we will suppose, and get up early in the morning determined to make a good day's march, and, while the cook is getting breakfast, send a man off to drive in the stock. The rest of the party strike the tents, make up the bundles, eat their breakfast, and then begin to wax impatient, and wonder what has become of the man and the beasts. Presently he comes in with the pleasant intelligence that three-fourths of the stock have left, that he cannot see them anywhere, and that the ground is so hard he cannot trail them. Off you all go, some on foot, others mounted on the remaining horses, and in two hours' time or so the runaways are found and driven in. It is needless to say that they had abandoned very fine pasture and wandered many miles to find grass not half so good.

Well, this delay has not tended to improve your temper, and then the beasts have to be caught, and that is no easy job, and a good deal of kicking and cursing takes place. At last they are all secured, and you proceed to pack.

A man stands on each side of the mule to be operated upon; the saddle, a light wooden frame, is placed on his back and securely girthed; and a long rope is looped into proper form and arranged on the saddle. The side packs are then lifted into position on each side of the saddle and tightly fastened; the middle bundle is placed between them, a few spare articles are flung on the top, a tent is thrown over all, and the load is ready to be secured. The rope is so fixed that the fall, as it were, is on one side and the slack is taken in on the other. Each man places one foot against the pack or the animal's ribs, and, throwing the whole weight of his body into the effort, hauls with all his strength upon the line; one pulling on the fall, the other gathering in and holding all the slack, like two sailors sweating down the jib-purchase. At each jerk the wretched mule expels an agonized grunt, snaps at the men's shoulders, and probably gives one of them a sharp pinch, which necessitates immediate retaliation. The men haul with a will, squeezing the poor creature's diaphragm most terribly; "nothing like clinching them up tight," as they say. Smaller and more wasplike grows his waist; at last not another inch of line can be got in, and the rope is made fast. "Bueno," cries the muleteer, giving the beast a parting spank behind, which starts it off, teetering about on the tips of its toes like a ballet dancer. The unfortunate beast has assumed the appearance and proportions of an hourglass, large at each end and exceedingly small in the middle. The apparent sufferings of that mule arising from undue compression of its digestive apparatus are pitiable to behold; but it is all "kid"; the heart of a mule is deceitful altogether, and in an hour's time that pack will require tightening again.

Having done with one animal, the packers proceed to the next, and so on through the lot. While you are busy with the others, Numbers One and Two have occupied themselves in tracing mystic circles in and out, among and round and round several short, stumpy, thickly branching firs, and, having with diabolical ingenuity twisted, tied, and tangled their trail-ropes into inextricable confusion, are standing there patiently in their knots. Number Three, on whose back the brittle and perishable articles have been entrusted, he being regarded as a steady and reliable animal of a serious turn of mind, has acquired a stomachache from the unusual constriction of that organ, and is rolling over and over, flourishing all four legs in the air at once. Number Four, who carries the bedding, a pack bulky but light, and measuring six feet in diameter has thought to run between two trees only five feet six inches apart, and, hopelessly jammed there, is trying vainly to back out stern first. She is a persevering creature, and in time backs herself out of the pack altogether. Numbers Five and Six, fidgeting and twisting about as only mules can do, come into violent and unexpected collision with each other behind, and with ears laid back and tails tucked between their legs are squealing and letting fly, as if they never expected to have another chance of kicking in this world. It is no use interfering; nothing will stop them. You may use language strong enough to split a rock, hot enough to fuse a diamond, without effect; you may lay hold of the trail-ropes and drag as hard as you like, but you might as well catch the tail end of an express train and expect to stop it. It is wiser to refrain from all active intervention, for possibly you may be kicked; certainly you will be knocked down and dragged about in a sitting posture, to the great destruction of your pants. You may, and of course you do, curse and swear your "level best"; but it does not do a bit of good. Go on they will, till they kick their packs off; and then they must be caught, the scattered articles gathered together, and the whole operation commenced afresh.

At last things are all fixed. Bottler leads off on his riding-horse, old "Billy," for the mules know him and will follow him anywhere; and the pack animals straggle after. We take a careful look over the place lately occupied by our camp to see that nothing is left behind; coil up our lariats, tie them behind the cantle, take our rifles, swing into the saddle, and spread out in open files, some behind, some on the flanks, to keep the cavalcade in order. All goes very nicely for a while; the beasts are plodding along, very slowly it is true, for some will wander, while others will stop to graze; when suddenly Satan enters into the heart of the hindermost animal. A wild ambition fires his soul; he breaks into a trot, and tries to pass to the front. A tin bucket begins jangling on his back; he gets frightened at the noise, and breaks into a canter. The bucket bangs from side to side; all the small articles in the pack rattle and shake; an axe gets loose, and the handle drops and strikes against his ribs; he fancies that there must be something alive upon his back hurting and belaboring him—something that must at any price be got rid of. A panic seizes him, and, wild with fright, he breaks into a mad gallop. Yells of entreaty, volleys of oaths are hurled at him; two of us try to cut him off, and only add to his terror and make matters worse. The pack begins to slip over his tail; mad with ungovernable fear, blind with terror, he kicks, squeals, and plunges. A saucepan flies out here, a lot of meat-cans there; a sack of flour bursts open and spills its precious contents over the ground; the hatchet, innocent cause of all the row, is dangling round his neck; a frying-pan is wildly banging about his quarters; until at last he bucks himself clean out of the whole affair and, trembling and sweating with fear, stands looking on the havoc he has wrought, and wondering what on earth the noise was all about.

A start very like that which I have attempted to describe above was made on leaving Bottler's ranch on Tuesday morning. Bottler led the way followed by the pack mules and the rest of the party. Many mishaps we had during that day's march of eight miles, and right glad we were to get into camp at the end of it.

Though the weather was still disagreeable, we got along much better on Wednesday, making a very fair march and camping comfortably on a little creek that discharges itself into the Yellowstone.

The next morning we started up the creek. We at first experienced some difficulty in making way. The creek bottom is quite impracticable and the animals could scarcely retain their foothold on the slippery grass.

Two or three tributaries discharge their waters into the principal creek, through small gulches and valleys. We wound our way towards the head of the valley, half asleep, for the day was very hot. Before long I jerked my horse on to his haunches and slid quietly off. The others followed my example without a word, for they too had caught a glimpse of the dark brown forms of some wapiti feeding quietly in the wood. Bottler, in his enthusiasm, seized me violently by the arm and hurried into the timber, ejaculating at every glimpse of the forms moving through the trees, "There they go! There they go! Shoot! Now then! There's a chance." At the time he was dragging me along, and I could no more shoot than fly. At last I shook myself clear of him, and, getting a fair easy shot at a large fat doe, fired and killed her.

Wapiti are the stupidest brutes in creation; and, instead of making off at once, the others all bunched up and stared about them, so that we got two more before they made up their minds to clear out. There was a fine stag in the herd, but, as is usually the case, he managed to get himself well among the hinds out of harm's way, and none of us could get a chance at him. Bottler and I followed his tracks for an hour, but could not come up with him; and, finding that he had taken clear up the mountain, we returned to the scene of action. There we found the rest of the party busily engaged in cutting up the huge deer. One of them was a hind, in first-rate condition and as fat as butter. We were very glad of fresh meat, and, as the ground was very suitable, determined to camp right there, and send some of the flesh down to the main camp in the morning. We pitched our Lilliputian tents at the foot of one of a hundred huge hemlocks, set a fire, and proceeded to make ourselves comfortable for the night.

We were all smoking round the fire—a most attentive audience, watching with much interest the culinary feats which Bottler was performing—when we were startled by a most unearthly sound. Bottler knew it well, but none of us strangers had ever heard a wapiti stag roaring before, and it is no wonder we were astonished at the noise. The wapiti bellows forth one great roar, commencing with a hollow, harsh, unnatural sound, and ending in a shrill screech like the whistle of a locomotive. In about ten minutes this fellow called again, a good deal nearer, and the third time he was evidently close to camp, so we started out and, advancing cautiously, we presently, through a bush, distinguished in the gloom the dark body and antlered head of a real monarch of the forest as he stalked out into an open glade and stared with astonishment at our fire. He looked perfectly magnificent. He was a splendid beast, and his huge bulk, looming large in the uncertain twilight, appeared gigantic. He stood without betraying the slightest sign of fear or hesitation; but, as if searching with proud disdain for the intruder that had dared to invade his solitude, he slowly swept round the branching spread of his antlers, his neck extended and his head a little thrown back, and snuffed the air. I could not see the fore sight of the little muzzle-loader, but luck attended the aim, for the bullet struck high up and a little to the back of the shoulder; and, shot through the spine, the largest wapiti stag that I had ever killed fell stone-dead in his tracks.

It was early in the season, and his hide was in first-rate condition, a rich glossy brown on the sides and jet black along the back and on the legs; so we cut off his head and skinned him; and, by the time we had done that and had packed the head and hide into camp, it was pitch dark, when we were ready for supper and blankets.

The accommodation at the Mammoth Hot Springs Hotel was in an inverse ratio to the gorgeous description contained in the advertisements of the Helena and Virginia City newspapers. No doubt the neighborhood of these springs will some day become a fashionable place. At present, being the last outpost of civilization, that is, the last place where whisky is sold, it is merely resorted to by a few invalids from Helena and Virginia City, and is principally known to fame as a rendezvous of hunters, trappers, and idlers, who take the opportunity to loiter about on the chance of getting a party to conduct to the geysers, hunting a little, and selling meat to a few visitors who frequent the place in summer; sending the good specimens of heads and skeletons of rare beasts to the Natural History men in New York and the East; and occupying their spare time by making little basketwork ornaments and knickknacks, which, after placing them for some days in the water so that they become coated with white silicates they sell to the travelers and invalids as memorials of their trip. They are a curious race, these mountain men, hunters, trappers, and guides—very good fellows as a rule, honest and open-handed, obliging and civil to strangers when treated with civility by them.

For a week we lay at the hot springs on Gardiner's River, unable to move on account of illness in the camp. The weather was beautiful; the storm had entirely subsided, and was succeeded by bright, warm, sunny days, softened and beautified by the dim autumnal haze. It was very aggravating to lose such fine weather for traveling, and we chafed impatiently at the enforced delay. Some of us went out hunting, and brought in good store of fat antelope; others amused themselves with the trout which abound in Gardiner's River and the Yellowstone. At last, on a Sunday we made a start.

In the afternoon we passed quite a patriarchal camp, composed of two men with their Indian wives and several children; half a dozen powerful savage-looking dogs and about fifty horses completed the party. They had been grazing their stock, hunting and trapping, leading a nomad, vagabond, and delicious life—a sort of mixed existence, half hunter, half herdsman, and had collected a great pile of deer-hides and beaver-skins. They were then on their way to settlements to dispose of their peltry, and to get stores and provisions; for they were proceeding to look for comfortable winter quarters, down the river or up the canyon.

The number of horses staggered us at first, but we soon discovered that the strangers were white, and, moreover, that there were only two men in camp; and without more ado we rode in and made friends. What a lot of mutually interesting information was given and received! We were outward bound and had the news, and the latitude and the longitude. They were homeward bound, had been wandering for months, cut off from all means of communication with the outside world, and had but the vaguest notion of their position on the globe.

But, though ignorant of external matters and what was going on in settlements, they had not lost all desire for information. An American, although he lives with an Indian woman in the forests or on the plains, never quite loses his interest in politics and parties; and these two squaw-men were very anxious to hear all about electioneering matters.

These men looked very happy and comfortable. Unquestionably the proper way for a man to travel with ease and luxury in these deserts is for him to take unto himself a helpmate chosen from the native population. . . . With an Indian wife to look after his bodily comforts, a man may devote himself to hunting, fishing, or trapping without a thought or care. He may make his mind quite easy about all household matters. His camp will be well arranged, the tent pegs driven securely home, the stock watered, picketed, and properly cared for, a good supper cooked, his bed spread out, and everything made comfortable; his clothes and hunting gear looked after, the buttons sewn on his shirt (if he has got any shirt—or any buttons) and all the little trivial incidents of life, which, if neglected, wear out one's existence, he will find carefully attended to by a willing and affectionate slave.

They had a lot to tell us also about their travels and adventures, about the wood and water supply, and the abundance or deficiency of game. So we sat down on bales of beaver-skins and retailed all the civilized intelligence we could think of. The women came and brought us embers for our pipes, and spread out robes for us and made us at home. Chubby children, wild and shy as young wolves, peered at us from behind the tent out of their round, black, beady eyes.

Soon after leaving their camp we crossed the low divide between the valley of Gardiner's River and that of the Yellowstone, and camped very late on Tower Creek, a little above its junction with the former river.

The falls, and also a portion of Tower Creek, are well worthy of a visit. The canyon of the river is exceedingly precipitous and rugged. Through this narrow gorge the river foams and rushes with great velocity; and about 200 yards above its entrance into the Yellowstone, which occurs just where that river debouches from the Grand Canyon, it shoots over an abrupt descent of 156 feet, forming a very picturesque fall.

The next day we broke camp early, and about noon met another party consisting of three men, out prospecting. They had but the haziest notion of their whereabouts in the world. They had wintered in the mountains, and had only once been into settlements, down somewhere on Snake River, early in the spring. We gave them all the information we could and bought some flour from them, giving them an order on Bottler's brother for some groceries in exchange.

We camped at a late hour on the south side of the mountain; and what a supper I did eat! It may seem strange, and it may be very shocking to think and talk about one's material comforts and gross appetites: but, as I am writing from memory whatever comes uppermost, the recollection of antelope-steak is very fresh and distinct just at present, savoring in my nostrils and bringing moisture to the lip, and overpowering all other thoughts. In fancy I can scent the odor of it afar off. Would that I could do so in reality! Bearing in mind that I had lived for a week at the hot springs on burnt flour and water, you will perhaps pardon my gastronomic enthusiasm. If people deny that one of the greatest enjoyments of life is eating when you are famishing, then those people either are devoid of the first principles of morality or have never been hungry; and they had better learn to speak the truth, or live on spare diet for a week, then get into vigorous health, and so know what a good appetite really means.

If a man wishes to be comfortable in camp, let him once and for all give up the idea of being too comfortable. If he tries to carry out his preconceived ideas as to cleanliness and dry changes of clothes; warm things for cold weather and cool garments for hot; boots for riding and boots for walking, and all the rest of the appliances of civilized life, he will find himself constantly worried and continually disappointed. . . . no, no; reduce yourself to primitive simplicity; one suit, and a change of undergarments. If it is cold, put on your change and extra shirt; if it is very hot, go without your coat or waistcoat or breeches, if it pleases you.

As with dressing so it is also with cooking. The same principle obtains in both cases; the simpler and less pretentious the style of your cook the better pleased you will be with the result of his efforts. . . . If you like to sit at a cloth spread and arranged in imitation of a dinner table and to eat of fried meat, very good; I don't mind. Those two candles that dimly illuminate you are very hard and solid; they are made of elk-fat; and before you have done supper you will have several of those candles in your inside. It is all a matter of taste.

Let me tell you the other way. First of all, make yourself a cake of flour and water, a little sugar, salt of course, and a pinch—a most minute pinch—of baking powder. It does not matter if you put none of the last ingredient in; the bread will be wholesomer without it. Roll this out extremely thin like a biscuit, score it with your knife, put it on a tin plate, and prop it up with a short stick before the embers to bake. It will be crisp, brown, and digestible in a few minutes. Put another plate near the fire, and let it get nearly red-hot. Then with a sharp knife cut yourself a portion of meat from the best part of the animal, cutting it at least an inch and a half thick. Beat it with your knife handle to break up the fiber, unless it is very tender indeed. Then divide it into several small fragments, one of which you will, after carefully salting and peppering it, impale upon a stick and plunge momentarily into a bright clear flame. Then toast it slowly over the embers. The sudden immersion in the fire glazes the surface of the meat and cakes the salt over it, so that during the after process of cooking scarcely any of the juice can escape, and the result is a kabob, rich, succulent, tender, and fit for any epicure. While you are eating one bit you toast another. Your plate is hot, your meat hot, your bread crisp and hot, and your tea hot; and, if that won't satisfy you in the wilderness, nothing will. This was my style and Bottler's; and we would lie side by side in front of the fire, toasting a little bit, and yet still another little bit, long after the others had bolted their hot soft rolls and fried meat.

We had a most lovely camp that night on the edge of a prairie, in a little cozy grassy bay that indented the forest shores. The sun sank in a quiet sky; the stars shone clear, bright, and steady with unwavering light; the universe rested and was at peace. The wind talked to the trees, and the pines in answer bowed their stately heads, and with a sigh of melancholy swept their gloomy branches to and fro. All through the night the mysterious music of the distant falls rose and fell upon the breeze—sometimes borne up distinct and clear, a mighty roar and crash of waters; then sinking to an almost inaudible hum like the tremulous vibration of a mighty but remote harp string. Not far away stood some bare burnt pine-trees, sadly complaining to the night air when it rose and softly touched their naked boughs, making to it their melancholy moan, and sinking again into silence as the breeze passed on.

We could hear the short comfortable crop, crop, crop of the horses as they nipped the herbage. The day had been very warm, and the air was heavy with the faint odor of autumn flowers and sweet grass, and with the strong fragrance of the resinous firs. It was almost too fine a night to waste in sleep, but slumber comes soon to tired men soothed by Nature's harmony when the elements are at rest; and unconsciousness, casting over us her mantle, quickly wrapped our senses in her dark folds.

Morning found us up betimes blowing our fingers and stamping our feet in that chilly "little hour before day," pulling up tent-pegs, rolling packs, putting together a few necessaries, and making preparation for a hard day's work. We intended, if possible, to pitch our tents the same evening beyond the Mud Springs, and to visit the Falls of the Yellowstone.

So after seeing everything properly packed and secured, we turned our horses' heads and, guided by the distant sound of water, cantered off, full of expectation, to see one of the greatest sights of the countryside, and after a short ride, we arrived at the river's brink just above the Falls.

Both the Falls are caused by basaltic dykes or walls, crossing the bed of the river at right angles to its course. The volume of water is not very great; and there is nothing stupendous or soul-subduing here as there is at Niagara; neither are the Falls very remarkable for their height. But they have a savage beauty all their own, a wild loveliness peculiar to them; and what they lack in volume, power, and general grandeur is amply atoned for in the preeminently distinctive character of the scenery about them, and by the lavish display of color and strange forms of stratification which distinguish their surroundings. The scene is so solitary, so utterly desolate, the coloring is so startling and novel, the fantastic shapes of the rock so strange and weird, that a glamour of enchantment pervades the place, which, though indelibly impressed upon my mind, is yet quite impossible to describe.

We were very soon hurried out, noticing the fact that the pine trees were casting short shadows, and that it must be getting very late into the forenoon. So we reluctantly went back to our horses, who had been eating all the time, and in nowise thinking of or appreciating the scenic excellence about them. Tightening up our girths, we swung into the saddle and resumed our way.

I never enjoyed a ride more in my life, and never expect to have so pleasant a one again. The day was very bright and warm, and the hazy autumn atmosphere cast over distant objects a shimmering gauzy indistinctness that greatly enhanced their beauty.

Meat had been growing very scarce for the last few days. We had scraped clean the bones of the antelope we packed with us from Gardiner's River, and afterwards boiled them into soup; and we had killed nothing on the march except wapiti stags, which at this time of year are not fit to eat; so we determined to halt, for a day at any rate, and endeavor to replenish the larder. Accordingly, the next morning before light, we all went out—each taking a different direction— to look for game; scanning the ground and peering through the trees, with the eagerness not only of hunters, but of hungry men. But no distant rifle-shot, bearing tidings of dinner, broke the silence of the morning air, or echoed "supper" through the glades, and about nine o'clock the hunters returned tired and dejected, all with the same story to tell; plenty of old sign, but not a single fresh track, and nothing whatever eatable to be seen. So we hurriedly broke camp and moved about five miles, to a little branch rising among some old beaver dams; and there pitched our tents again, it being the last water to be found on the north side of the divide which separated us from the Firehole Basin.

Our path lay for some distance along the verge of an old lake bed, now a grass-covered prairie; and then striking into the timber, it crossed a low divide into the valley system of the Firehole, or east fork of the Madison River. . . . The trail runs for the most part along the Firehole River, the water of which is warm, and apparently much appreciated in cold weather by flocks of geese and ducks. It is fed by numerous little streams, the beds and sides of which are brightly colored and so variegated that they present sometimes an appearance almost of rough mosaic. In some the water is very hot, hot enough to make the mules hop when they tread in it. In others it is comparatively cool, varying in temperature according to the distance the water has run from the boiling source.

The streams and river are lined with very dense green vegetation. The sides of the river, in fact, the whole face of the country, is honeycombed and pitted with springs, ponds, and mud-pots; furrowed with boiling streams, gashed with fissures, and gaping with chasms from which issue hollow rumblings, as if great stones were rolling round and round or fierce, angry snarls and roars.

The ground sounds hollow underfoot. The trail winds in and out among holes that puff sulphur fumes or squirt water at you; by great caverns that reverberate hideously and yawn to swallow you up, horse and all; crosses boiling streams which flow over beds composed of a hard crust, colored yellow, green, and red; and skirted by great cisterns of boiling, bubbling, seething water. The crust feels as if it might break through at any moment and drop you into fire and flames beneath, and the animals tread gingerly upon it.

When we arrived, the "Castle" was placidly smoking. Far down in the depths of the funnel an indistinct rumbling could be heard, but it seemed quite inactive. However, a couple of men belonging to another party, who had been there some days, told us that they expected it to spout about eleven at night; so we set to work to make ourselves comfortable in camp.

Scarcely had we got things fixed and supper under way, when a yell from Bottler, "He's going to spout!" caused us to drop teapot and pannikin, and tumble out of the tent in half no time.

It was getting dark, but there was quite enough light to see that the fit was upon the imprisoned monster. We ran upon the platform, close to the crater, but were very soon driven from that position and forced to look on humbly from a distance.

Far down in his bowels a fearful commotion was going on; we could hear a great noise—a rumbling as of thousands of tons of stones rolling round and round, piling up in heaps and rattling down again, mingled with the lashing of the water against the sides as it surged up the funnel and fell again in spray. Louder and louder grew the disturbance, till with a sudden qualm he would heave out a few tons of water and obtain momentary relief. After a few premonitory heaves had warned us to remove to a little distance, the symptoms became rapidly worse; the row and the racket increased in intensity; the monster's throes became more and more violent; the earth trembled at his rage; and finally, with a mighty spasm, he hurled into the air a great column of water.

I should say that this column reached at its highest point of elevation an altitude of 250 feet. The spray and steam were driven through it up to a much greater elevation, and then floated upward as a dense cloud to any distance. The operation was not continuous, but consisted of strong, distinct pulsations, occurring at a maximum rate of seventy per minute; having a general tendency to increase gradually in vigor and rapidity of utterance until the greatest development of strength was attained, and then sinking again by degrees. But the increase and subsidence were not uniform or regular; the jets arose, getting stronger and stronger at every pulsation for ten or twelve strokes, until the effort would culminate in three impulses of unusual power.

The column of water appeared quite perpendicular, and was constantly ascending, for long before one jet had attained its greatest elevation, another had been forced through the aperture; but in the column the different efforts were plainly visible. The volume of water ejected must have been prodigious; the spray descended in heavy rain over a large area, and torrents of hot water six or eight inches deep poured down the sloping platform.

The noise of the eruption was indescribable. I know of but one simile drawn from Nature that conveys the smallest impression of it, and even then the impression is quite inadequate to illustrate the subject. Have you ever sat upon the very verge of a steep sea-cliff in a gale? I don't mean one of your yachtsman's breezes, but a real bona fide full winter's gale of wind, roaring from the north-west over leagues and leagues of white Atlantic, and striking full against the cliff-face. If you have, you will know that there is at the edge a little space of complete calm, where the pinks are scarcely stirred, and where you can sit and listen to the awful riot around you, untouched by it. If you will sit there, and are unaccustomed to such a scene, you will be half deafened and quite frightened by the strife of wind and rock and sea. Hear with what tremendous blows the gale strikes against the bold front of cliff and flies hoarsely howling with rage just over your head! Listen to its vicious scream, as, baffled, it beats against the crags, and shrieks shrilly round some jutting rock! The ground seems to shake under the shock and thunder of the breakers against its base; and under all you will note the continuous hollow roar of the pebble bank crumbling to the sea with each receding wave. To all these sounds of elemental war add the shrieking of the steam pipes of many steamers blowing off, and you will have some idea of an eruption of the Castle.

Or, if you don't know much about the sea, you may imagine a gigantic pot boiling madly with a thunderstorm in its stomach, and half full of great stones rolling and knocking about against its reverberating sides. Taken with the above-mentioned steam-pipe accompaniment which is indispensable, this may convey a faint idea of the noise.

The total display lasted about an hour. Water was ejected for twenty minutes, and was then succeeded by steam, which was driven out with much violence and in great quantities. Like the water, it was expelled in regular beats, increasing in rapidity as the jet decreased in strength until the pulsations merged into one continuous hoarse roar, which gradually but fitfully subsided, and the exhausted geyser sank back into complete repose.

To enjoy such a sight as this, a man should have time to get a little accustomed to it, for the display of such stupendous force exhibited in such an unusual manner is, to say the least of it, startling.

In our case, the grandeur and awfulness of the scene were intensified by the darkness, for before the eruption ceased night had fallen, and obscurity enshrouding the plain rendered even common objects unnatural and strange. From out a neighboring vent white puffs of steam were forced, which, bending forward in the light breeze, crept slowly past the mound, looking in the dark like sheeted ghosts stooping under the burden of their crimes. The grey plain, and, the naked pines stretching out their bared arms menacingly like warning spirits, showed ghastly in the half-light; and with these accompaniments of darkness and novelty, and amid a confused noise and concussion of the atmosphere, and shocks and trembling of the earth, this great geyser was exhibiting a spectacle entirely new and strange to all of us except one of the party.

We considered ourselves very lucky to have so soon seen one of the principal geysers in action; and damp but happy we went to bed.

The next morning broke very dull. Dense columns of steam rose heavily from innumerable vents into the still morning atmosphere. The air was filled with smothered indistinct noises emanating from the various springs and smaller geysers.

After breakfast we walked up to the head of the valley and, taking our stand upon the mound of Old Faithful, took a general survey of the basin. Old Faithful is so called because he plays faithfully every three-quarters of an hour. Old

Faithful is not to be compared with the Castle, but it is a very fine geyser. When in operation it displays a great amount of vigor; and it presents unusual facilities for observation, for, if a man does not object to standing up to his ankles in water (and if he does, he had better remain at home) he can, by keeping windward on a breezy day, stand within a foot or two of the orifice during the period of eruption.

We left this extraordinary district with great regret: fain would we have tarried longer in it. An opportunity for exploration such as none of us had ever before enjoyed was most temptingly displayed, and very gladly would we have availed ourselves of it. Four years ago the white world knew absolutely nothing of the country we were leaving. The few legends of Indian tribes, and the vague rumors of hunters that occasionally came to the surface and were wafted out from the wilderness to the ears of civilized men, were entirely disbelieved, or were looked upon as fables built on the very smallest foundation of truth. And even now scarcely anything is known about it. A few parties go in from Virginia City and out at Bozeman, all following the same trail, examining the same objects, halting at the same places. They never stray any distance from the usual route, and there are hundreds of valleys into which no human foot has ever burst, thousands of square miles of forest whose depths have never yet been penetrated by the eye of man.

It is extremely improbable that the area of volcanic activity is confined to the limited space occupied by the two Geyser Basins, and it is very possible that other depressions may be found containing springs and geysers as great as, or even more important than, those I have attempted to describe. The scenery is beautiful, the climate most healthy; game is abundant, and every lake and river teems with trout. It is a district affording infinite scope to the tourist in quest of novelty, the hunter, or the scientific traveler.

The stock of information concerning it as yet acquired is extremely small, and, with the exception of the compilations of the various government expeditions, the accounts are untrustworthy and inaccurate. Very anxious were we to add our mite to the general fund in the way of something newly discovered and observed; but winter was drawing nigh, and, as we had no mind to be blocked in to the southward of Mount Washburn we returned reluctantly to our camp.

It had been our intention to go from the Firehole Basin down the Madison to Virginia City, thus making a round trip of it, and obviating the necessity of passing the same ground twice; but, owing to our stock being so poor and in such bad condition, we were compelled to abandon this idea and take the back track home: for though the distance from the geysers to Virginia City is shorter than that to Fort Ellis, we knew that by adopting the latter route we could, if necessary, get fresh animals at Bottler's. We found our camp all right, so far as the bipeds were concerned, except that they were hard up for food, for the country had produced no game.

The day after our return we packed up and marched to Tower Falls, arriving there many hours after dark.

We rode to the Mammoth Hot Springs. Our outfit was getting exceedingly demoralized, and on this occasion also it was long after dark before we got into camp. We had counted upon getting plenty of game, deer or elk, all through the trip, and had arranged the commissariat accordingly. But we had grievously miscalculated either our own skill or the resources of the country, for not an atom of fresh meat had we tasted for days. This sort of perpetual fast began to tell upon us. We were a hungry crowd.

Trout I had devoured till I was ashamed to look a fish in the face. A trout diet is all very well in warm weather, and taken with moderate exercise; but when the mercury gets below freezing, and you have to work hard all day, commend me to venison and fat pork. So not only were the horses and mules tired and sulky, but the humans also were beginning to show signs of dissatisfaction. Bottler and I formed ourselves into a committee of supply and started off ahead of the column, determined to get some food to eat.

We rode all the morning without seeing a single solitary creature fit to eat. In the afternoon we crossed the trail and went up on some high bluffs overlooking the cascade on Gardiner's River. It was blowing so hard, and there was such a noise of storm that there was no danger of the shot having disturbed anything. As the country looked very gamey, we walked on foot, leading the horses, and presently came upon a little band containing six antelopes. We were by this time near the summit of a long sloping mountain. The ground fell away rapidly on either side, and in a long but narrow glade the antelope were lying. While we were peering at them, two does—nasty inquisitive females—got up, walked forward a few steps and stared too. We remained still as statues, and after a while they appeared satisfied and began to crop the grass. We then left our ponies and hastened up under cover of some brush. By the time we reached the tree nearest to them we found the does had all got up and fled to some distance, but a splendid buck with a very large pair of horns was still lying down. At him I fired, and nailed him. He gave one spring straight into the air from his bed, fell back into the same spot, kicked once or twice convulsively, and lay still.

We saw a great many antelope that day; but as we were now close to the end of our journey, and our horses moreover were so beat that it would have been unwise to give them any extra work to do, and as the day was scarcely long enough for the journey we had to make, we did not take the trouble to try and kill anything.

We therefore made the best of our way along our old trail, galloping cheerily over the level, and walking and driving our horses before us over all the steep places; keeping a look-out for Indians, but not troubling our heads about game. Just about sunset we passed the corral, and saw that most marvelous old dame, Mrs. Bottler—marvelous for the sprightliness with which she bears the burden of her many years—busily engaged milking her cows, a sight that was highly refreshing and suggestive of luxurious feeding. A few minutes afterwards we pulled up at the ranch and were heartily greeted by Phil Bottler, who warmly bid us to get right off, and sit right down, and not trouble ourselves about the stock, for he would manage all that. He put out chairs for us, called in his mother, and went out to drive our tired horses down to pasture. What a refreshing wash we had! And how we did enjoy our supper of fresh eggs, chicken, cream, butter and cheese, and plenty of Japan tea! Honestly tired we were, and heartily glad to have got to the end of our troubles.

We had brought to a safe termination a most enjoyable expedition, the pleasant recollections of which will never fade from my memory; but we had also experienced a somewhat rough time. Our horses and mules were scarcely up to the work; we had been greatly hurried; we were unfortunate as regards the weather, and still more unlucky in not getting half enough game to keep us properly supplied. So the pleasures of the trip were mixed up with just enough hardship to make the return pleasant.

It was a stormy day on which, with great regret, we left Fort Ellis and the pretty little town of Bozeman. It was snowing heavily and bitterly cold when we drove into Virginia City, where we remained two days, and then took the stage to Corinne.

EMMA COWAN

—◆—

Emma Cowan and her husband, brother, and sister visited Yellowstone National Park in 1877—the year the U.S.
Army pursued the Nez Perce Indians through the park. The
Nez Perce generally had amicable relations with whites, but
in what has become a familiar story, the peace was shattered
when gold was discovered on Indian land. Some Nez Perce
acquiesced to government demands to move to a tiny reservation, but others decided to flee their homeland instead.

The army sent soldiers to subdue the defiant Nez Perce, but
the Indians defeated them several times. In the most dramatic
defeat, the army made a predawn attack on the sleeping Nez
Perce camp on the banks of the Big Hole River in southwest
Montana. The Nez Perce rallied, drove back their attackers,
and then retreated, leaving their equipment, teepees, and at
least eighty-nine dead—many of them women and children.

After the battle they fled though Yellowstone Park, an
unexpected move because people thought Indians feared
the geysers. After making their way through the rugged Yellowstone wilderness, the Nez Perce discovered they were not
welcome with their old friends the Crow, who had made an
accommodation with the whites. Then they headed north in
hopes of joining Sitting Bull and his Sioux in Canada. In
October the starving and exhausted remnants of the band
surrendered to the army just forty miles from the Canadian
border. Mrs. Cowan died in Spokane, Washington, in 1938.

Emma Cowan's memoir is one of the gems of Montana literature. It was originally published in 1903 in Contributions to the Historical Society of Montana *and has been republished many times. The following is a condensed version.*

CAPTURED BY INDIANS—1877

From Emma Cowan's memoir

In Virginia City, where we lived the first year in Montana, 1864–1865, my father one day brought home an old man who told us some very marvelous stories. My father termed them fish stories; however, I enjoyed them immensely. My fairy books could not equal such wonderful tales—fountains of boiling water, crystal clear, thrown hundreds of feet in the air, only to fall back into cups of their own forming—pools of water within whose limpid depths tints of the various rainbows were reflected—mounds and terraces of gaily colored sand—these and many others were the tales unfolded.

Although we enjoyed his stories, for he told them well, we considered them merely the fantasy of his imagination. Still I gleaned from them my first impression of Wonderland. As I grew older and found truth in the statements, the desire to someday visit this land was ever present.

In 1875 I was married, and in 1877 occurred our memorable trip to the park and capture by the Nez Perce Indians. We were told that the Indian is superstitious. The phenomena of the geysers very probably accounts for the fact that this land is not now and never has been Indian country. A few Indian trails are found within the boundaries of the park as they are in other parts of the West. Yet this year the Indians were very much in evidence in the national park, as we found to our sorrow.

***This photo shows Emma Cowan and her husband in 1905
at the site where they were captured by Nez Perce Indians
nearly thirty years before.***
Pioneer Museum of Bozeman photo

We were thankful, however, that it was the Nez Perce we
encountered, rather than a more hostile tribe, as they were
partially civilized and generally peaceful. Yet at this day,
knowing something of the circumstances that led to the final
outbreak and uprising of these Indians, I wonder that any of
us were spared. Truly a quality of mercy was shown us during
our captivity that a Christian might emulate, and at that time
when they must have hated the very name of the white race.

Deprived of their reservation, on which they had lived
years without number, and because they rebelled and
refused to sign a treaty giving up the last remnant of this
land, hunted and hounded and brought to battle, wounded

and desperate, fleeing with their wives and children to any land where the white man was not—yet they were kind to us, a handful of the hated oppressors. Think of it, you who assume to be civilized people! Less than ten days had elapsed since the Big Hole fight in Montana, in which women and children, as well as warriors, were killed by the score. A number, badly wounded, were in camp while we were there. Yet were we treated kindly, given food and horses, and sent to our homes.

The summer of 1877 my brother Frank told us of his intention to visit the park, and asked us to be in the party. It required but little effort on his part to enthuse us, and we soon began preparations for the trip.

I induced my mother to allow my young sister, a child of little more than a dozen years, to accompany me, as I was to be the only woman in the party and she would be so much company for me. The party consisted all told of the following persons: A. J. Arnold, J. A. Oldham, and a Mr. Dingee, all of Helena, Mr. Charles Mann, my brother Frank Carpenter, Mr. Cowan, my sister, myself, and a cook named Myers.

We were nicely outfitted with an easy double-seated carriage, baggage wagon, and four saddle horses—one of them my own pony, a birthday gift from my father years before, which I named Bird because she was trim and fleet. That I was fond of her goes without saying. We were well equipped in the way of provisions, tents, guns, and, last but not least, musical instruments. With J. A. Oldham as violinist, my brother's guitar, and two or three fair voices, we anticipated no end of pleasure.

We left Radersburg the sixth of August, camping the first night at Three Forks. Our way lay up the Madison via

Henry's Lake, a road having been built to the Lower Geyser Basin from that direction. Although some parts of this would scarcely pass as a road, we traveled it without mishap. The second day's ride brought us to Sterling, a small town in Madison County.

The next noon found us at Ennis, and twelve miles farther up the Madison for our night camp. We passed the last of the ranches that afternoon. At Ennis my husband had been told we would find fishing at Henry's Lake—also boats, spears, skeins and all sorts of tackle. The man, to whom they belonged, however, was at one of the ranches cutting hay, but he would give us a key to the boathouse if we could find him. Inquiring at the ranch to which we had been directed, we found that he had gone to another, five miles distant. My disappointment may be imagined for my fancy had run riot and I fully expected to see the old man of the tales of my childhood. A horseback ride of a few miles obtained the key, but my curiosity was not gratified then or afterwards.

In the afternoon two days later we left the Madison River, up which we had been traveling, and crossed a low divide, getting our first glimpse of the lake. The view from this point is exceedingly pretty. Some of the pleasantest days of our trip were spent here. Innumerable flocks of wild fowl have their home in this isolated spot. Low marshy land encircles the greater part of this lake, but where the houses are built the ground is much higher, giving a fine view of the lake and surrounding hills. The immense spring affords a sufficient stream of water to float a boat through the marsh and out to the lake

Torchlight fishing by night was a unique pastime. Great schools of fish, attracted by the glare of light from 100 blazing pine knots, gathered about the prow of the boat. Some fine ones were speared and delicious meals enjoyed.

The following morning we broke camp and continued our travel. We passed to the southeast and crossed Targhee Pass, then through ten miles of pine barrens, and camped again on the Madison River at the mouth of the canyon.

Our last camp before reaching the Lower Basin was at the junction of the Gibbon and Firehole rivers, these two forming the Madison. Not a soul had we seen save our own party, and neither mail nor news of any sort had reached us since leaving the ranches on the Madison.

Leaving the Gibbon fork after dinner, we traveled several miles of low foothills and entered the Lower Geyser Basin. We had at last reached Wonderland. Mr. Cowan insisted always on making camp before doing anything else, putting up tents, gathering fragrant pine bows for camp beds, getting things in regular housekeeping order. But this day our first sight of the geysers—with columns of steam rising from innumerable vents and the smell of the inferno in the air from the numerous sulphur springs—made us simply wild with the eagerness of seeing all things at once.

My small sister and I could scarcely keep pace with the men, but we found enough to interest us, turn where we would. I recalled and told to her many of the tales told me of this weird land in earlier years. How vividly they came to mind!

The next day we established a permanent camp near the Fountain Geyser, and made daily short excursions to the different points of interest. We explored every nook and cranny of the Lower Basin and were ready for pastures new.

We had reached the terminus of the wagon road. As we could go no farther with the wagon, we decided to leave our camp intact, only taking the few things necessary for a few days' stay in the Upper Basin, and go horseback. This we did, and pitched our tent that night in a point of timber, very close to Castle Geyser, which by way of reception gave us a night eruption, covering us with spray and making a most unearthly noise.

At dawn we circled around the crater, too late to see more than great columns of steam. We saw the geyser in eruption several times while in the basin, but by daylight it did not seem so terrifying. The Giantess was not in eruption during our stay of five days. We enjoyed the Grand, considering it rightly named. In the meantime, my brother, with some others in the party, had gone to the fall and Yellowstone Lake. We remained five days in the Upper Basin and arranged to meet the others on the 22nd in the Lower Basin.

Thursday, the 23rd of August, found us all at the home camp, as we termed it, ready to retrace our steps towards civilization. We had a delightful time, but were ready for home. This day we encountered the first and only party of tourists we had seen, General Sherman and party. They had come into the park by way of Mammoth Hot Springs. Of them we learned of the Nez Perce raid and the Big Hole fight.

We also received the very unpleasant impression that we might meet the Indians before we reached home. No one seemed to know just where they were going. The scout who was with the General's party assured us we would be perfectly safe if we would remain in the basin, as the Indians would never come into the park. I observed, however, that his party preferred being elsewhere, as they left the basin that same night.

That afternoon another visitor called at camp, an old man by the name of Shively, who was traveling from the Black Hills and was camped half a mile down the valley. Home seemed a very desirable place just at this particular time, and we decided with one accord to break camp in the morning, with a view of reaching home as soon as possible. Naturally we felt somewhat depressed and worried over the news received.

My brother Frank and Al Oldham, in order to enliven us somewhat, sang songs, told jokes, and finally dressed up as brigands, with pistols, knives, and guns strapped on them. Al Oldham, with his swarthy complexion, wearing a broad sombrero, looked a typical one, showing off to good advantage before the glaring campfire. They made the woods ring with their nonsense and merriment for some time.

We probably would not have been so serene had we known that the larger part of the audience consisted of the Indians, who were lurking out in the darkness, watching and probably enjoying the fun. The advance party of Indians had come into the basin early in the evening. Before morning the entire Indian encampment was within a mile of us, and we had not heard an unusual sound, though I for one slept lightly.

I was already awake when the men began building the campfire, and I heard the first guttural tones of two or three Indians who suddenly stood by the fire. I peeped out through the flap of the tent, although I was sure they were Indians before I looked. I immediately aroused my husband, who was soon out. They pretended to be friendly, but talked little.

After some consultation the men decided to break camp at once and attempted to move out as though nothing unusual was at hand. No one cared for breakfast save the Indians, who quickly devoured everything that was prepared. By this time twenty or thirty Indians were about the camp, and more coming. The woods seemed full of them.

Some little time was required to pull down tents, load the wagons, harness and saddle horses, and make ready to travel. While Mr. Cowan was engaged elsewhere one of the men—Mr. Arnold, I think—began dealing out sugar and flour to the Indians on their demand. My husband soon observed this and peremptorily ordered the Indians away, not very mildly either. Naturally they resented it, and I think this materially lessened his chances to escape.

We drove out finally on the home trail, escorted by forty or fifty Indians. In fact they all seemed to be going our way except the squaw camp, which we met and passed as they were traveling up the Firehole towards Mary's Lake. A mile or more was traveled in this way, when the Indians for some reason called a halt. We were then a few hundred yards from where the road enters the timber and ascends the hillside.

One of the Indians seated on a horse near Mr. Cowan, who was also on horseback, raised his hand and voice, apparently giving some commands, for immediately forty or fifty Indians came out of the line of timber, where they evidently had been in ambush for our benefit. Another Indian addressing Mr. Cowan was pointing to the Indian who had given the command, and said in good English, "Him Joseph." And this was our introduction to that chief.

Every Indian carried a splendid gun, with belts full of cartridges. As the morning sunshine glinted on the polished surface of the gun barrels, a regiment of soldiers could have not looked more formidable. We were told to backtrack, which we did, not without some protest, realizing however the utter futility. The Indians pretended all the while to be our very good friends, saying that if they should let us go, bad Indians, as they termed them, would kill us.

Passing and leaving our morning camp to the right, we traversed the trail towards Mary's Lake for two miles. We could go no farther with the wagons on account of fallen timber. Here we unhitched, mounted the horses, taking from the wagon the few things in the way of wraps that we could carry conveniently, and moved on.

After traveling some ten miles, a noon camp was made, fires lighted, and dinner prepared. Poker Joe (we did not learn the Indian name) acted as interpreter. He talked good English, as could all of them when they desired. Through him we were told that if we would give up our horses and saddles for others that would be good enough to take us home, they would release us and we would be allowed to return to the settlement without harm. Many of their horses were worn out from the long hurried march. Under the circumstances we acquiesced, and an exchange began.

I was seated on my pony, watching the proceedings, when I observed that two or three Indians were gathering around me, apparently admiring my horse, also gently leading her away from the rest of the party. They evidently wanted the animal and I immediately slipped out of the saddle to the ground, knowing that I would never see my pony again, and went to where Mr. Cowan was being persuaded that an old rackabone gray horse was a fair exchange for his fine mount. He was persuaded.

Poker Joe told us we could go. We lost no time in obeying the order. All went well for us for a half-mile or so. Then to our dismay we discovered Indians following us. They soon came up and said the chief wanted to see us again. Back we turned, passed the noon camp, now deserted, and up and on to higher timbered ground. The pallor of my husband's face told me he thought our danger great.

Suddenly, without warning, shots rang out. Two Indians came dashing down the trail in front of us. My husband was getting off his horse. I wondered what the reason. I soon knew, for he fell as soon as he reached the ground—fell heading downhill. Shots followed and Indian yells, and all was confusion. In less time than it takes to tell it, I was off my horse and by my husband's side, where he lay against a fallen pine tree. I heard my sister's screams and called to her. She came and crouched by me, as I knelt by his side. I saw he was wounded in the leg above the knee, and by the way the blood spurted out I feared an artery had been severed. He asked for water. I dared not leave him to get it, even had it been near.

I think we both glanced up the hill at the same moment, for he said, "Keep quiet. It won't last long." That thought had flashed through my mind also. Every gun in the whole party of Indians was leveled at us three. I shall never forget the picture, which left an impression that years cannot efface. The holes in those gun barrels looked as big as saucers.

I gave it only a glance, for my attention was drawn to something near at hand. A pressure on my shoulder was drawing me away from my husband. Looking back over my shoulder, I saw an Indian with an immense navy pistol trying to get a shot at my husband's head. Wrenching my arm from his grasp, I leaned over my husband, only to be roughly drawn aside. Another Indian stepped up, a pistol shot rang out, my husband's head fell back, and a red stream trickled down his face from beneath his hat. The warm sunshine, the smell of blood, the horror of it all, a faint remembrance of seeing rocks thrown at his head, my sister's screams, a faint sick feeling, and all was blank.

After coming to my senses my first recollection was of a great variety of noises—hooting, yelling, neighing of horses— all jumbled together. For a while it seemed far off. I became conscious finally that someone was calling my name, and I tried to answer. Presently my brother rode close to me. He told me later that I looked years older and that I was ghastly white. He tried to comfort me and said the Indians had told him no further harm would befall us. It seemed to me the assurance had come too late. I could see nothing but my husband's dead face with the blood upon it. I remember Frank's telling me my sister was safe, but it seemed not to impress me much at the time.

The Indians soon learned that my brother was familiar with the trail, and he was sent forward. Over this mountain range, almost impassable because of thick timber, several hundred head of loose horses, packhorses, camp accouterments, and five or six hundred Indians were trying to force a passage.

The wearisome uphill travel was at length accomplished. Beyond the summit the timber was less dense, with open glades and parks. Finally, at dusk we came to a quiet valley, which had already begun to glow with campfires, though many were not lighted until sometime later. The Indian who was leading my horse—for I had been allowed to ride alone after recovering consciousness, the Indian retaining a grip on the bridle—threaded his way past numerous camp fires and finally stopped near one.

As if by a prearranged plan someone came to the horse, enveloped in a blanket. Until he spoke I thought it to be an Indian, and I was clasped in the arms of my brother. Tears then, the first in all these dreary hours, came to my relief. He led me to the fire and spoke to an Indian seated there, who I was told was Chief Joseph.

He did not speak, but motioned me to sit down. Frank spread a blanket on the ground, and I sat down on it, thoroughly exhausted. A number of squaws about the fire were getting supper. My first question had been for my sister. I was told that she was at Poker Joe's camp, some little distance away, together with the old man Shively, who was captured the evening before.

My brother and I sat out a weary vigil by the dying embers of the campfire, sadly wondering what the coming day would bring forth. The Indian who had befriended him told him we would be liberated and sent home. But they had assured us a safe retreat the day previous and had not kept faith. Near morning, rain began falling. A squaw arose, replenished the fire, and then came and spread a piece of canvas across my shoulders to keep off the dampness.

At dawn, the fires were lighted, and soon all was activity, and breakfast under way. Only a short distance away, which I would have walked gladly the night before, I found my sister. Such a forlorn child I trust I may never again see. She threw herself into my arms in a very paroxysm of joy. She seemed not to be quite certain that I was alive, even though she had been told.

Poker Joe again made the circle of the camp, giving orders for the day's march. We were furnished horses, and my brother came up leading them that morning. We reached the crossing of the Yellowstone near the mud geysers at noon. The Indians plunged into the stream without paying much regard to the regular ford, and camped on the opposite shore. We watched the fording for some time, and finally crossed.

At the squaw camp dinner was being prepared. I began to feel faint from lack of food. I forced down a little bread, but nothing more. Fish was offered me, but I declined with thanks. I had watched the squaw prepare them something this wise. From a great string of fish the largest were selected, cut in two, dumped into an immense camp-kettle filled with water, and boiled to a pulp. The formality of cleaning had not entered into the formula. While I admit that tastes differ, I prefer having them dressed.

A council was being held. We were seated in the shade of some trees watching proceedings. Six or seven Indians, the only ones who seemed be in camp at the time, sat in a circle and passed a long pipe one to the other. Each took a few whiffs of smoke, and then one by one they arose and spoke. Poker Joe interpreted for us. Presently he said the Indians had decided to let my sister and me go together with the soldier who had been captured that morning, but would hold my brother and Shively for guides. I had not been favorably impressed by the soldier. Intuition told me he was not trustworthy, and I refused to go unless my brother was also released. This caused another discussion, but they agreed to it, and preparations were made for our departure. A search was made for my saddle, but without avail. It was later found by some of Howard's soldiers near where Mr. Cowan was shot.

Some of our bedding, a waterproof tarp, a jacket for my sister, bread, and matches, and two old worn-out horses were brought, and we were ready. We clasped hands sadly with our good friend Shively, promising to deliver some messages to friends in Philipsburg, should we escape. His eyes were dim with tears. In reality, I considered his chances to escape better than ours and so told him. The Indians needed him for a guide. "We may be intercepted by warriors out of camp," I said. "No," he replied, "something tells me you will get out safely."

We crossed the river again, my brother riding behind Poker Joe, who went with us a half mile or more, showing us presently a well-defined trail down the river. He told us we must ride, "All night. All day. No sleep." We could reach Bozeman on the second day. He reiterated again and again that we must ride all night. We shook hands and set out very rapidly. My brother walked and the horses we rode were worn out. It seemed folly to think we could escape. Furthermore, we placed no confidence in the Indian. I regret to say that as soon as he was out of sight we left the river trail and skirted along in the timber.

After several miles of travel in this way, we came to a valley through which we must pass to reach the trail down by the falls. We decided to wait on a timbered knoll overlooking the valley until the darkest part of the night, so that we might cross without being seen by the Indians. The moonlight was so bright that it was two o'clock or more before we attempted it. After crossing nearly halfway, we came to a washout, or cut, over which we could not jump the horses. It seemed to me hours before we finally came to a place where we could cross, so that before we gained the shelter of the timber once more, it was broad daylight.

We passed down the river, leaving to our left the mountain pass over which the Indians had brought us the day before. We dared not retrace that route, even though my husband lay dead there—dead and unburied, perhaps dragged and torn by wild beasts. My own peril seemed of little consequence, compared to the cruel agony of this thought. We passed the falls. I was familiar with the route from this point. I was sure we would find friends nearer than Bozeman, as Poker Joe had said. We would find them at the Mammoth Hot Springs.

About noon the sign that someone was ahead of us was apparent. In crossing streams, pony tracks in the wet sand were plainly seen, and the marks of rope or lasso that had been dragged in the dust of the trail indicated Indians. They often drag the rope thus, I am told. We passed Tower Creek and stopped a very short time to rest the horses. A few hours later, in rounding a point of timber, we saw in a little meadow not far beyond, a number of horses and men. At first glance we thought them Indians. Frank drew our horses back into the timber and went forward to investigate. He returned in a very few minutes and declared them soldiers. Oh, such a feeling of relief!

Imagine their surprise when we rode into the camp and my brother told them we were fleeing from the Indians, the only survivors of our party, as he believed then. The soldier we had left at the Nez Perce camp the day before was a deserter from this company. Retribution closely followed transgression in his case. Mr. Shively escaped after being with the Indians ten days, but the fate of the soldier we did not learn.

The company of soldiers was a detachment from Fort Ellis, with Lieutenant Schofield in command. They were sent out to ascertain the whereabouts of the Nez Perce and were returning in belief that the Indians were not in that vicinity. Of them we learned that General Howard was closely following the Indians. Many of their actions were thus accounted for.

The soldiers kindly prepared supper for us. I remember being nearly famished. Camp had been made for the night, but was quickly abandoned, and arrangements made for quick travel. We were mounted on good horses, and the poor old ones that had done us good service, notwithstanding their condition, were turned out to graze to their heart's content.

This night, unlike the previous one, was dark and cloudy. We passed over some of the roughest mountain trails that I ever remembered traveling. Many of the soldiers walked and led their horses. Near midnight we reached Mammoth Hot Springs, tired and stiff from long riding, but truly thankful for our escape.

I found, as I anticipated, some acquaintances, and strangers as well as friends who did everything possible for our comfort. Two Englishmen with their guide were about to make a tour of the park. One of these men was a physician and kindly assisted in dressing wounds. I am certain he never found a time when his services were more appreciated.

A semi-weekly stage had been run to the springs that season. We were told that if we desired we could rest till Wednesday and return to Bozeman on that stage. On Monday, Mr. [Henry "Bird"] Calfee invited us to go to Bozeman with him. He said he had a pair of wild mules and a big wagon, but if we wished, he would take us. We were anxious to get home and very glad for so good an opportunity. The Englishmen and their guide also decided to return to Bozeman. Wonderland had lost its attractions for the nonce.

A long day's ride brought us to the Bottler ranch on the Yellowstone. Mr. Calfee decided to remain there a day or so. His photographic supplies were somewhat shaken, likewise his passengers. We found excitement rife at this point. Chief Joseph and his band were expected to raid every section of Montana at the same moment apparently. The Crow Indians, whose reservation is just across the Yellowstone River, extending miles up and down, took advantage of this fact, and numerous horse-stealing raids occurred, for which the Nez Perce received credit.

In the afternoon of the next day a friend drove out from Bozeman, and we made twelve of the forty-mile drive that evening, remaining in the Ferril home on Trail Creek all night. They received us kindly, and though their own family was large, they made room for us. A sitting room was converted to a bedroom, and camp beds made down for several children.

During the evening we gave them the details of our encounter with the Indians. To them, Indian scares were common. Living so close to the Crow reservation, they were always on the alert and never felt quite safe. The children listened with great interest, telling us afterward what they would do, should they be captured. They knew where to dig for camas root, and they would escape to the brush and live on that.

We had only gotten settled for the night when a neighbor came tapping at the door, telling us to get up quickly and dress, as Indians were about. Such a scrambling for clothes in the dark! A light was not to be thought of. A regular mix-up of children and clothes occurred, which the mother alone could straighten out. The little folks seemed rather to enjoy the excitement. Several shots were exchanged, but the Indians, who were undoubtedly Crows on a horse-stealing raid, as soon as they found themselves discovered, disappeared. We retired again, but did not sleep much.

We drove to Bozeman next day. A few miles from the town we met seventy or eighty Crows, escorted by Lieutenant Doane on their way to intercept the Nez Perce. They looked rather more dangerous than any we had met. After reaching Bozeman, my brother eventually went with this party nearly to Mammoth Hot Springs in his endeavor to reach the point where Mr. Cowan was shot, but he was compelled to return again to Bozeman without accomplishing that result.

In the meantime I had reached my father's home. Kind friends and neighbors had kept the news of our capture from my people until the day we reached home, then prepared them for our coming, thus sparing them much of the suspense. I reached there worn out with excitement and sorrow. Years seemed to have passed over my head since I had left my home a month previous.

From the time I learned of the close proximity of General Howard's command to the Nez Perce at the time Mr. Cowan was shot, I could not but entertain a faint hope that the soldiers might have found my husband alive. Yet, in reviewing all the circumstances, I could find little to base such a hope on. Still, as one after another of the party were accounted for, all living, the thought would come. I believed I should know to a certainty when my brother returned from his quest.

I had been home a week when one afternoon two acquaintances drove to the house. My father not being in, I went to the door. They would not come in, but talked a few minutes on ordinary subjects. Then one of them handed me a paper and said news had been received of Mr. Cowan that he was alive.

In the "Independent" Extra I found this account:

COWAN ALIVE.
HE IS WITH GENERAL HOWARD'S COMMAND.

Special to the Independent—Bozeman, September 5. Two scouts just in from Howard's command say that Cowan is with Howard and is doing well and will recover. He is shot through the thigh and in the side and wounded in the head. Howard was fourteen miles this side of Yellowstone Lake.

Some way the doorstep seemed conveniently near as a resting place just at that particular time. Presently they told me the particulars. He was badly wounded, but would live, was with Howard's command, and would either be sent back to Virginia City or brought the other way to Bozeman. For the time being, this news was all sufficient. A day or two passed. I learned nothing more. My brother Frank came but had the same news only that had been given me. The hours began to drag. I decided to go to Helena with my brother, as from that point telegraphic news could reach me much sooner. After arriving in Helena, however, a whole week passed before a telegram came to me, stating my husband would be in Bozeman the following day.

I lost no time going. At Bozeman, however, I found that he had given out at the Bottler ranch on the Yellowstone. A double-seated carriage was procured for the trip, and once again I found myself traversing the familiar and oft-traveled road. But this day the sun shown. My husband had notice of my coming and was expecting me. I found him much better than I dared anticipate, and insistent on setting out for home without delay.

We arranged robes and blankets in the bed of the carriage. With his back propped up against the back seat, he was made quite comfortable. We stopped for a handshake and congratulations at the Ferril home on Trail Creek. We had a rather spirited team and made fair progress. Late in the afternoon we were at a point seven miles from Bozeman, in Rocky Canyon. The road was graded around a steep hillside for some distance. We could look down and see the tops of trees that grew on the stream far below. Presently we experienced the novel and very peculiar sensation of seeing our carriage resting on those same trees, wheels uppermost, and ourselves a huddled mass on the roadside. A broken pole strap caused the carriage to lunge forward of the horses as it ran up against them. The buggy tongue caught, snapped and threw the carriage completely over. Fortunately the seats were not fastened and we were left—a bundle of seats, robes, blankets, and people on the hillside—shaken but not much hurt. The carriage, from which the horses had freed themselves, made one revolution as it went over and landed as described. We were thankful to have left it at the first tip.

Mr. Cowan was lifted to a more comfortable position by the roadside. Not long after, a horseman leading a pack animal came along. Our driver borrowed the horse, making the trip to Fort Ellis and back in the shortest possible time and returning with an ambulance. Seven miles seemed long ones, and before we reached Bozeman Mr. Cowan was almost exhausted, his wounds bleeding and needing attention. He was carried by careful hands to a room in the hotel as soon as the crowd had thinned out somewhat. Mr. Arnold arranged to dress the wounds, and in order to do so, seated himself on the side of the bed, when lo, the additional weight caused the whole inside of the bed to drop out and down on the floor. This sudden and unexpected fall, in his enfeebled state, nearly finished him. A collapse followed, from which he did not rally for some time.

A week passed before we were able to travel farther. By the time we reached home Mr. Cowan was able to hobble about on crutches. The winter passed, however, before he was entirely well. A severe gunshot wound through the hip, a bullet hole in the thigh, a ball flattened on the forehead, and the head badly cut with rock. Few, indeed, are the men who could have survived so severe an ordeal.

Many years have passed since the events herein narrated occurred, yet retrospection is all that is needed to bring them to mind clear and distinct as events of yesterday—many years, since which life has glided on and on, with scarce a ripple beyond the everyday sunshine and shadow that falls to the lot of each and all of God's people.

JACK BEAN

—◊◊◊—

As word spread about the abundant wildlife at Yellowstone, trophy hunters began arriving from the east and Europe. But even if the trophy seekers were skilled hunters, they needed someone to guide them through the unfamiliar and rugged West. Jack Bean was the perfect man for the job. Before becoming a guide, Bean was a trapper, hunter, and Indian fighter.

In the summer of 1877, the army hired Bean to look for Chief Joseph and the Nez Perce Indians who were fleeing their homelands in Idaho and Oregon to avoid being forced onto a tiny reservation. Bean searched in the park and along the Madison River but didn't find any Indians, apparently because they had already moved on.

He returned to Bozeman after the futile quest and discovered that a Colonel Pickett wanted to hire him as a hunting guide. Bean, in his memoir, doesn't provide much information about Colonel Pickett—not even a first name. But he did say Pickett had seen a bear only once and was eager to kill one. Pickett, whose first name was William, was from Alabama and a colonel in the Confederate Army. As Bean comments, he later became a famous bear hunter.

At the time, Montana newspapers were filled with stories about the Nez Perce defeating the army in several battles and capturing and killing tourists in Yellowstone National Park, and people said the colonel was foolish to want to go to the

park. But he insisted, and Bean, who thought the Nez Perce
had left the area, agreed to take him.

Later Bean built a homestead in the Bridger Canyon
near Bozeman and used it as headquarters for his business
as a packer and hunting guide. Over the years his customers
included the government geologist and explorer Ferdinand
Hayden and the wealthy British financier William Black-
more. Although he wasn't a member of the nobility, Black-
more was often called "Sir" or "Lord."

In 1900 Bean moved his family to California and in 1902
went into the tire business in San Jose. He worked there until
his death in 1923. He wrote his memoirs with a pencil in
tire store ledger books, and his family donated them to the
Pioneer Museum in Bozeman, where they remain. Bean was
a natural storyteller, but he indulged in strange syntax, cre-
ative spelling, and a mountain man's penchant for tall tales.
The excerpts below have been edited extensively.

HUNTING, FISHING, AND
GEOLOGIZING—1877

From Jack Bean's memoir

When I reached Bozeman, General Willson, who owned and operated the leading mercantile store in Bozeman, asked me if I would go back through the Yellowstone National Park. I advised him that I would if there was anything in it for me.

He said an old gentleman visited his store nearly every day and tried to induce him to go. But Willson, being a businessman instead of a mountaineer, was not willing to accompany the man. Willson really doubted if the man would go; he thought the request merely a bluff as it was thought that there were straggling Indians all through the country.

So Willson arranged a meeting. In the evening, I went down to his store, and Willson introduced me to Colonel Pickett and told him I knew the country and would go through the park with him. The Colonel showed considerable excitement but was too blooded to back out.

So plans were made to go, and in a couple of days we started. We journeyed over to the Yellowstone and up to the Mammoth Hot Springs. The people that we saw told us we were fools to undertake the trip. We found blood all over the cabin down at the hot springs where the Indians had killed a man.

We didn't get but a little way more before we found a dead horse and pack where the Indians had attacked a man, but he

Jack Bean was a trapper, scout, and Indian fighter before he went into the business of guiding hunters to Yellowstone Park.
Pioneer Museum of Bozeman photo

succeeded in getting into the brush to save himself. We only went a few miles farther until we found another dead horse where two scouts and an Indian boy (whom we thought came from Howard's Expedition) were attacked in the night. One horse was killed and the two white men got away, but the Indian boy was never heard of afterwards. The country was getting more interesting for the Colonel, but we kept going.

Passed the mouth of the East Fork of the Yellowstone and in going up a hillside trail I heard a big owl hoot up on top. It made me think of Indians around, and I told Colonel Pickett if they made a break, to get into the brush, which was down in the bottom of the gulch. There was nothing left for us to do but go on. When we got to the top of the hill I saw the prettiest bird in all my life, a big owl. This convinced us that it was a real owl instead of decoying Indians.

We camped on Tower Creek at night. The Colonel was very anxious to kill a bear and had only seen a bear entering the brush on his previous hunting trips.

The next morning our trail led us over Mount Washburn, where it commenced to snow. By the time we had reached our highest point in the trail the snow was about a foot deep. As the Colonel had only summer shoes, he had to walk to keep warm. So the Colonel stopped to dig the snow off his shoes and tie them a little tighter. I looked back behind me and saw a big bear crossing the trail. I spoke to the Colonel, "There goes a bear"—but he kept tying his shoe. When he had finished, he raised his head and with a southern accent answered me, "Whar?"

I advised him that a bear didn't wait for a man to tie his shoe. Our trail now left the ridge and descended down to the head of Tower Creek, where we saw another big bear in the trail coming toward us. So I told the Colonel, "There comes a bear."

"Whar?" he answered, so I showed him. He got off his horse and walked quietly up the trail. I watched Mr. Bear and saw him leave the trail and start up the grassy hillside.

I was afraid that the Colonel would shoot him when the bear was right above him and it would come down and use him rather roughly. The Colonel saw him when he was on the hillside about thirty yards away, so I dismounted and slipped up behind the Colonel. When the Colonel shot the bear it made a big growl and came down the hill on the run and passed him within thirty feet. The Colonel didn't know I was so close behind him until I spoke.

I told him to hold his fire until the bear jumped the creek, but he wouldn't do it. As the bear passed, the Colonel shot and missed him. When the bear crossed the creek I opened fire with my Winchester. By the time the Colonel could load and was ready to shoot again I had put five Winchester balls into him. But the Colonel gave him his last shot through the breast while the bear was falling. It rolled into the creek dead.

We found when we had examined the bear that the Colonel's first shot just went under the skin in the bear's neck, which caused him to come down the hill so rapidly. I knew that the Colonel would want to take this hide along. But we only had one packhorse between the two of us and it was too loaded to carry the wet and green hide. So I decided that I had better spoil it. So I gave my knife a lick on the steel and as we got to the bear stuck my knife between the ears and split the skin down the backbone clean to the tail.

The Colonel gave me a slap on the back and says, "Bean, that's my bear."

I told him, "All right." It was no credit to me to kill a bear.

"Well," he says, "We'll take this skin."

I said, "Why didn't you say so before I split the skin, why I've spoiled it."

The Colonel was very much put out to lose the skin. He tramped the snow down for ten feet around and finally concluded he would take the front paw and hind foot and a good chunk of meat to eat. I only took meat enough for him, as I didn't care for bear meat. And after dissecting the bear we journeyed on our way to the Yellowstone Falls and made camp.

That night he wanted me to cook him plenty of bear meat, but I cooked bacon for myself. I noticed him after chewing the bear meat a little would throw it out of his mouth when he thought I wasn't looking. I gave him bear meat for about two days and throwed the balance away, which was never inquired for.

We went over to the Lower Geyser Basin and got there quite easily and put the evening in looking at the geysers and paint pots. The next day we went up to the Upper Geyser Basin and saw close to the Castle Geyser, where thirty Nez Perce Indians had slept a few nights before.

After viewing the geysers until we were satisfied, we journeyed down the Firehole River, which is the headwaters of the Madison. We saw so many fresh pony tracks that it made us a little anxious. What puzzled us was we didn't see any ponies.

When we got through the Madison Canyon we made camp quite early and I had the Colonel go back to the mouth of the canyon and watch there until sundown. In the meantime, I had packed up everything, saddled the horses, and when the Colonel came in just at sundown we put the packs on.

As the Madison made a big detour around, we struck straight through the timber to the Madison Basin on our night drive. We went about six miles, came into quite a big band of antelope that got up out of the prairie. That convinced us there were no Indians around there. So we unpacked and unsaddled, made our beds, and had a good sleep.

The weather had moderated considerable, and there was no snow here, which made traveling much easier. So in the morning we went down to the east fork of the Madison and had breakfast. After breakfast we packed up and journeyed on down the Madison and struck the settlements the next evening.

In the next three days we reached Bozeman and that concluded the trip with Colonel Pickett. Pickett remained in the country and became a great bear hunter, killing as high as four bears in one day.

Dr. Hayden, the American geologist, came to Bozeman and got up a party to go through and geologize what we now know as Yellowstone National Park.

I was his guide and packer for this trip, and after getting everything in readiness at Fort Ellis we went over to the Yellowstone River and traveled a short distance up the canyon past Cinnabar Mountain to Mammoth Hot Springs.

Hayden gave his young men students their orders in the morning to scale certain mountains, take the altitude, and catch a few bugs. One of the men fetched in a little lime crystal and asked Dr. Hayden if it was of any interest. He said it was of great interest and to bring in all curious things we found.

I told him I knew where there were crystals that were blue, and he complimented me by telling me I was a liar. But I finally interested him enough to send a party and see for themselves. I told Dr. Hayden that we would pass not far from the blue crystals so he detailed a little party with Dr. Peale in charge to go and explore my big mountain story.

Dr. Hayden asked me if I knew what blue crystals would be, and I told him they would be just what I called them— "blue crystals."

He said, "You fool—they would be amethysts."

While the Doctor was geologizing the country there, I went fishing with Sir William Blackmore. You could plainly see plenty of trout close to the shore of the lake. When he got to catching them, he thought it would be wonderful if he caught one for each year he was old—fifty-four. He soon caught the fifty-four and tried for a hundred. He was not long making this and tried for fifty-four more—and kept fishing for another hundred—and another fifty-four.

As we had gotten two thirds of the way around the lake by this time, I told him I would quit as I had all the fish I could drag along the grass, being two hundred and fifty-four. I dragged them to camp and wanted to make a little show of these fish.

Sir Blackmore, whenever he would see any bones, would ask: "How come those bones there?" I would tell him they were left by skin hunters in the winter. He thought that all skin hunters should be put in jail for such vandalism. I told him he would do the same if he were in this country in the winter.

So when I had shook all these fish off from the strings they made such a sight that I called Dr. Hayden's attention to what Sir Blackmore would do if he had a chance. Hayden colored up considerable and excused Blackmore by saying: "The fish are so plentiful; it was a godsend to thin them out."

When we got back to the main camp—lo and behold—there were nine mule loads of blue amethysts, which we shipped back to the Smithsonian Institute.

From this camp we went up to Yellowstone Lake and then down to the Lower Geyser Basin. There we commenced to geologize and examine the hot springs and geysers. With fishing nets Hayden's students could reach into these springs, pick out little round formations from the size of shot to hen's eggs, which they called geyser eggs. They got so many of these specimens that I took about ten loads to Virginia City, a distance of seventy-five miles. These were also shipped to the Smithsonian Institute.

We brought back supplies to the main camp, about a three-day trip. We passed into the canyon of Bridger Creek, down to the Three Forks and then back to Bozeman to disband. Dr. Hayden and his students returned to Washington, D.C.

CARRIE ADELL STRAHORN

—ᴍ—

Carrie Strahorn was an adventurous woman who refused to stay at home when her husband, Robert ("Pard" as she called him) went on scouting trips for the Union Pacific Railroad. The Strahorns got free train passes, but Pard's job was to look for places far from transcontinental tracks that the company could promote as destinations. That meant they had to travel long distances by stagecoach.

In 1880 the Strahorns visited Yellowstone National Park, where they met George Marshall and his wife. The Marshalls built the first true hotel in the park, and Mrs. Marshall had the first white baby born there. They also met Philitus Norris, Yellowstone's second park superintendent. Carrie Strahorn presents Norris as a bit of a buffoon, so perhaps it's no surprise that he erroneously told her that she was the first person to take a complete tour of the park. Historians generally say that Emma Stone, who visited the park in 1874, deserves that credit.

Nonetheless, Carrie's description of her adventures in Yellowstone is an excellent story. The following is an abridged chapter from her 1911 book, Fifteen Thousand Miles by Stage.

AN OCTOBER SNOWSTORM—1880

From Carrie Adell Strahorn's book
Fifteen Thousand Miles by Stage

In the fall of 1880 my husband, Pard, and I made our first trip into Yellowstone Park—that land without a peer in the known world. The dear ones at home were in constant fear that we would starve or freeze, or a thousand other things that can arise in a parent's heart. Many Virginia City citizens begged us not to take the trip so late in the fall as early snowstorms were too hazardous and too severe to allow the trip to be made safely. But the plans had been carefully in progress for some weeks, and with the hour at hand for the trip we could not be persuaded to yield such a privilege. We would take our chances and trust in God and good horses.

The Marshall and Goff State Company sent the first public conveyance into the park, 120 miles distant, and we were to be the first passengers. With the best of drivers in Mr. Marshall himself, and Pard and I as the only occupants of the stage, at just daylight of October 1, 1880, we heard the wheels go round and soon were whirling merrily along the Madison Valley.

We had a sumptuous breakfast in the tidy log cabin of Gilman Sawtell, who was a Yellowstone Park guide. Then on to the top of Raynolds Pass from which point the "Three Tetons" rose before us in all their grandeur. Soon the island-dotted waters of Henry's Lake claimed all attention with its deeply indented shores and mountain guardians 3,000 feet high.

The deep green of the pine trees in contrast with the autumnal foliage lent a rare charm to the five miles of waterway.

The stage drew up to quite a pretentious building on the lakeshore about half past eight in the evening. But enthusiasm weakened when a nearer view of the house revealed no doors or windows, but in their places strips of canvas flapping over the openings.

The house was without furniture except a few cooking utensils, an old stove, a pine table, and some crude stools to sit on. Mr. Marshall made himself busy trying to get supper from supplies that had been brought from his house in the Lower Geyser Basin. He said he was awfully glad I could eat beans, but it was a case of mustard or beans, and the mustard was out, so there was not much choice.

After supper Pard and I gathered our blankets to go back to the stage to fix a place to sleep, but Mr. Marshall insisted there was a nice lot of hay upstairs where we could be more comfortable. He handed us a candle and directed us to a stairway. It was a rickety passage, with the wind howling through every aperture. Once upstairs, the room to which we were sent seemed about forty feet square. Our glimmering candle would light only a corner of the great black space that seemed full of spooks and goblins.

Pard had persuaded me to buy a very heavy pair of shoes in Virginia City, because the ground was so hot in some sections of the park that thin soles were not at all safe to wear. Then he had proceeded to hold them up to ridicule all day. I finally wagered five dollars with him that in spite of their looks I could get both of my feet into one of his shoes. So there in the dim candlelight, I called to him to bring me his shoe, and let me win my wager.

I put on his number seven and declared my foot was lost and lonesome in it, and he cried out, "Well, then, now put in the other one! Put in the other one!" I began at once taking it off to put it on the other foot, when he cried out, "Oh, no, not that way, but both at once."

But I revolted and said, "No, that was not in the bargain; I had not agreed to put both in at the same time."

In deep chagrin he threw a five-dollar gold piece at me, which was lost for half an hour in the hay before I could find it. And so we went on with our merrymaking, trying to forget our surroundings. It was a glad hour that saw us started again on our way with a new sun.

Leaving Henry's Lake our course was almost due east into the park. It was not until darkness settled around us that we reached the Lower Geyser Basin, at the entrance of which stood the new and unfinished little log house built by Mr. Marshall. It was with a twinge of disappointment that we were obliged to retire without seeing a geyser, but needing rest we were soon tucked away for the night and locked in slumber.

Next morning there was an early review of our surroundings; the log house was far from being finished, and the part we occupied was partitioned off with a canvas wagon cover. The second floor was only partly laid, and a window or two was missing in the upper part. The unfilled chinks between the logs allowed the rigorous October breezes to fan us.

In the frosty morning air the steam was rising from every point of vision and the whole ground seemed to be on fire, for boiling springs and geysers were almost without number. The first point to visit was the cluster of springs two miles from the hotel. The road was through fine meadowland and groves, and beside a rippling stream that was fed only by the overflow of the springs in question.

The first one reached was known as the Thirty Minute Geyser as that is the interval of time between its eruptions. It was getting ready to spout when we arrived and it gurgled and groaned and spouted a little; then after it dashed up in the air some twenty feet and sustained its height for three minutes. A quarter of a mile away the Queen Laundry Geyser covered an area of at least an acre and a half. The main basin of the Laundry was not over fifty feet across, but it flowed down in a series of pools nearly half a mile from its source and there became cool enough to bathe in, and to do laundry work.

The boiling pots close by had overflowed until they built around themselves huge walls some thirty feet high. Nearly all the geysers and boiling springs in the park have funnel-shaped craters, or apertures, with curiously formed linings of their own deposits. The waters are a dark blue and green and so clear that the walls and shelved sides could be seen as clearly at a depth of forty feet.

Leaving the Lower Basin, we followed up the east bank of the west fork of the Firehole River with geysers all along until we reached the big springs or geyser lakes, where we crossed the river and drove up to a level. The place was rightly named "Hell's Half Acre." As I looked into the black depths, when the breeze blew the fumes from us, the groaning of the waters was heard like evil spirits in dispute. The surface of the Half Acre measured 250 feet in diameter.

The spring had no period of eruption and it was not seen in its greatest glory until 1886 when visitors to the park who happened to be in the vicinity witnessed a rare spectacle. It was named the Excelsior Geyser because it is undoubtedly the most powerful geyser in the world. It suddenly broke out about three o'clock one Friday afternoon and continued to play twenty-four hours.

The witnesses pronounce it the grandest and most awe-inspiring display ever beheld. The spoutings were heard several miles distant, while the earth in the immediate vicinity was violently shaken as if by an earthquake. The noise of escaping steam and the internal rumbling were deafening. An immense body of rumbling, deafening water, accompanied by steam, was projected to an altitude of about three hundred feet, and the Firehole River, which is only a few rods distant, soon became a torrent of boiling water. The display was kept up, with gradually decreasing force, until the Excelsior went back to its normal state.

Above the Half Acre we crossed back to the east side of the river and found a spring boiling up through an old hollow stump. It stood so close to the river that the waters washed it slightly on one side. The stump was three feet high, and the water boiled constantly two feet above the top of it, directly through the heart of the stump, which was gradually becoming petrified.

Without waiting to examine the hundred or more geysers on our way, we continued up the river to the Riverside and Fan Geysers, where we again forded the stream and continued on until we reached the Castle Geyser, where we pitched our camp. The Castle seemed to be making a terrible fuss about something. Its crater looked more like a lighthouse than the ruins of a castle; it was indeed beautiful and majestic.

Above the Castle was Old Faithful, so called because of its perfect regularity, for every hour it throws the spectator into ecstasies of delight. It is so regular in time of spouting that it has often been called the "Big Ben" of the park, after the famous old Westminster clock of London. One hundred and fifty feet it threw its column of water six feet in diameter, and held it unbroken sometimes for ten minutes, and never less than five minutes.

We returned to our horses and moved our camp for the night farther down the stream to a little point of timber between the Grotto and the Giant. Both of these latter-named geysers showed signs of eruption, and while partaking of our supper the former seemed greatly agitated. We dipped the dishes in a hot spring close by and they were washed and wiped at the same time. The dome of the Grotto was remarkable. Over the centre of the main opening an arch obstructed direct passage of the water. The force with which the water had been thrown back on the sides of the cave had worn great holes through the walls, forming a half dozen or more orifices through which water poured with great force.

We had no tents, and with only the stars for a canopy we lay in the midst of the greatest wonders of the world—with a roar like many storms and battalions of artillery breaking the quiet air. With the ground for a mattress and pine boughs for a pillow we passed the night in waiting, listening and sleeping, by turn, but withal we rested our tired limbs and made ready to endure the fatigues still ahead of us.

The morning after our return from the Upper Geyser Basin, our party, including Mr. Marshall, Pard, and myself, started for the Mammoth Hot Springs in a light wagon. It was necessary to make it a two-day trip because of the numerous points of interest along the way—and also because of the horrible road. There are no adjectives in our language that can properly define the public highway that was cut through heavy timber over rolling ground, with the stumps left from two to twenty inches aboveground, and instead of grading around a hill it went straight to the top on one side and straight down on the other; whereas a few hundred dollars, properly expended, would have made it one of the finest drives in the world.

We had to abandon the light wagon and returned for a new start on horseback, for it was impossible to get any conveyance over the stumpy road. It was the only attempt at a road in the park, and what had been done with the government funds was pretty hard to see. The trails in the park, with one or two exceptions, were very difficult to follow and we often lost our way.

Soon we were trotting along to the Norris Plateau, or Norris Geyser Basin. This plateau embraced twenty-five square miles and seemed to be not only the most elevated and largest, but may also have been the most important and doubtless the oldest geyser basin in the park. It certainly was the hottest and most dangerous for pedestrians. The first little joker we reached was the Minute Geyser, and with an orifice of only a few inches it spurted up some five feet every sixty seconds, and then died down and showed not a ripple on its placid surface until it spurted again on time without any warning. To the right of the Minute Geyser was the Mammoth Geyser, and well it deserves its name. When it is quiet one can go up to the crater and study its beaded chimney, and look down its long dark throat, and shudder. Its chimney was about four feet high, with an orifice two feet by three feet in diameter. Its voluminous outbursts have fairly disemboweled the mountain at whose base it stands for a distance of a hundred feet or more, and at least forty feet in width, while its greatest depth that can be seen does not exceed twenty feet.

A few miles beyond the Norris Basin we passed the base of Obsidian Mountain, which looms up like a sheet of glass. Its shiny surface gives many colors in sunlight, including black, brown, yellow, and red. Every little splinter has the same glassy appearance as the mass.

The Mammoth Hot Springs of the Gardner River were at last in sight, after a very long, hard pull over a mountain, where several times we felt riveted to the spot, unable to go another step from sheer exhaustion.

The gorge in which the Mammoth Springs are located is over 1,200 feet above the level of Gardner River. From the river up there are fourteen terraces, and the largest and hottest springs are near the top. The waters have rolled down and deposited their lime until they have built huge bowls, or reservoirs, one after another. The limestones, which dip under the river, extend under the hot springs and are doubtless the source of lime noticed in the waters and deposits on the terraces as they are secure and firm. There is so much lime that it gives the whole earth a white appearance, while the inside of these natural bathtubs seem to be porcelain lined, and the water is a beautiful blue white. The outside crusting is rough and uneven with stalactites in profusion, which in some instances united with the stalagmites from the terrace below.

Each level or terrace has a large central spring, and the water bubbling over the delicately wrought rim of the basin flows the declivity, forming hundreds of basins from a few inches to six to seven feet in diameter and often seven feet in depth. The main terrace has a basin thirty by forty feet across, and the water is constantly boiling several inches above the surface: but a careful approach will permit one to peep into the reservoir and get a glimpse of the mossy vegetable matter that lines its sides in a rich light green that constantly waves with the ebullition of the water, and as the blue sky is reflected over all it lends an enchantment that no artist can duplicate.

Our attention was called to a monument some fifty feet high and twenty feet in diameter. No one was able to give any reason for its existence. The top was shaped like a cone and on the very summit was a funnel-shaped crater, which would lead one to believe that it had once been an active geyser, but it bore the significant title of "Liberty Cap."

On the terrace just above Liberty Cap is a fountain known as the "Devil's Thumb." I poked my head into one of the many large caverns which had once been boiling reservoirs, and inhaled the sickening fumes of Hades. I not only expected to see his Satanic Majesty's thumb but his entire self as well, and could fancy he would drag me in and carry me down for his dinner.

The sky was full of threatening clouds the morning that our little party started out with saddle and pack animals for the upper Yellowstone River. We followed the same old Indian trail that General Howard and his troops did three years before, and although there had not been a dollar spent on the road it was the only respectable trail in the whole park. For miles we rode along the east fork of the Firehole River, and then began a slow but steady ascent of the Rockies' main range.

After starting on this climb we saw what seemed to be a flying centaur coming rapidly toward us, but it proved to be the wings of Colonel Norris' greatcoat flying in the wind as he rode madly down the trail. We had missed him at the Mammoth Springs, and now he insisted upon retracing his steps and making one of our party. He started ahead over a trail so plain that a child could not lose it—the only visible trail we had found. Every half mile he told us not to worry about getting lost as he would keep in the lead and there was no danger. Colonel Norris was the superintendent of the park.

Darkness had settled when we reached the Yellowstone River and we hastened into camp. Pard had been commissioned to get an elk on a neighboring hill and Colonel Norris rode ahead to select the camp. Mr. Marshall and I rode more until the colonel called us to the camp of his selection.

Instead of selecting a place under good trees, he had stopped in the middle of an opening on a side hill. The rain began to fall almost as soon as we were out of the saddles. Pard had come in without his elk, and betokened a dismal night. The beds were made at once and covered with canvas to keep them as dry as possible. I longed for something good to be brought out of the mess chest, but it was the same old bread and bacon, and the same old excuse from Mr. Marshall, but a ride of thirty-five miles made us glad to get even that.

After supper we stood around the fire to dry our clothing, but as fast as one side was dry another side was wetter than ever, and thus we kept whirling around as if on a pivot until we gave up and went to bed, wet to the skin. We were lulled to sleep by the deep, sonorous voice of Colonel Norris, who forgot to stop talking when he went to sleep and he was still talking right along when we woke up at midnight.

The rain changed to snow, and through the storm we saw the disconsolate face of Mr. Marshall, as he stood near the smoldering campfire muttering to himself as if he had become demented. Upon our inquiring the cause of his trouble, he said that as soon as he saw the snow he went to look for the horses—and they were gone.

"Gone!" we all exclaimed in unison and despair. The horses were gone and we were at the end of our rations with a big storm upon us. The many warnings not to go into the park so late went buzzing through our minds like bumblebees. The snow was several inches deep and falling faster every minute.

As soon as daylight came, the men started in search of the horses. I was left all alone in the camp for several hours waiting with my rifle in hand, until after a hard and hurried chase the horses were overtaken and brought back. We knew that we should hurry home as quickly as possible—but to be within five miles and not to see the falls was asking too much. With the return of the horses we resolved at once to go on.

Superintendent Norris thought it was not best for me to go to the falls. The trip must be a hasty one, and the start home not to be delayed longer than possible for fear of continued storm. The snow ceased falling soon after daylight, but the sun did not appear and there was every indication of more snow. Pard was reluctant to leave me and knew what disappointment lurked in my detention, but he was overruled. With Mr. Norris he started off, leaving me with Mr. Marshall—who was to have everything ready for the return to Firehole Basin on their return.

The more I meditated the more I felt that I could not give up seeing the canyon and falls. To be balked by a paltry five or ten miles was more than I could stand. I called to Mr. Marshall to saddle my horse at once for I was going to the falls.

He laughingly said "all right," but he went right on with his work and made no move toward the horse. I had to repeat the request the third time most emphatically and added that I would start out on foot if he did not get my horse without more delay.

He said I could not follow them for I would not know the way, but I reminded him of the freshly fallen snow, and that I could easily follow the trail. He was as vexed with my persistence as I was with his resistance, and he finally not only saddled my horse but his own, and rather sulkily remarked that if the bears carried off the whole outfit I would be to blame. When well on our way I persistently urged him to return to the camp and he finally did turn back, but waited and watched me until I turned out of sight.

Alone in the wild woods full of dangerous animals my blood began to cool, and I wondered what I should do if I met a big grizzly who would not give up the trail. The silence of that great forest was appalling, and the newly fallen snow made cushions for the horse's feet as I sped noiselessly on. It was a gruesome hour, and to cheer myself I began to sing, and the echoing voice coming back from the treetops was mighty good company.

The five miles seemed to stretch out interminably. When about a mile from the falls other voices fell on my ear, and I drew rein to locate the sound, then gave a glad bound forward for it was Pard on his way back. Mr. Norris said anyone might think that Pard and I had been separated for a month, so glad were we to see each other.

Pard could not restrain his joy that I had followed, and sending the superintendent on to the camp he at once wheeled about and went with me to the falls and canyon that I came so near missing. Up and down o'er hills and vales we dashed as fast as our horses would carry us; the upper falls were reached, where we dismounted and went up to the edge of the canyon to get a better view.

The upper falls are visible from many points along the canyon, and the trail runs close to them and also by the river for several miles, giving the tourist many glimpses of grandeur. Above the upper falls, the river is a series of sparkling cascades, when suddenly the stream narrows to thirty yards, and the booming cataract rushes over the steep ledge a hundred and twenty feet and rebounds in fleecy foam of great iridescence. The storm increased and the heavens grew darker every hour, but we pushed on.

Moran has been chided for his high coloring of this canyon, but one glimpse of its rare, rich hues would convince the most skeptical that exaggeration is impossible. We longed to stay for days and weeks and hear this great anthem of nature and study its classical and noble accompaniment, but there was a stern decree that we must return, and that without delay.

There was no hope for sightseeing as we kept on our way back to the Lower Geyser Basin. Without giving our horses or ourselves over half an hour to rest at noon, we rode on and on, up hill and down, through woods and plains, until at last the lights of Marshall camp were in sight. The storm had continued all day, turning again from snow to rain in the valley. How tired I was when we rode up to the door. Our forty-mile ride was ended at seven o'clock, but it took three men to get me off my horse.

We left the park with the hope of spending a longer season there at an early day as there were many places of interest that we had to lightly pass and perhaps many that we did not see at all. There is not a section of the park that has not its peculiarities. Dr. Hayden estimated that there are ten thousand boiling springs and spouting geysers in that strange region.

With beds on the hard ground and little over us but the stars, with modest fare to work on, and blind trails to follow, the trip through the park was in marked contrast to the elegant coaching trip of the present day, where boulevards lead the traveler to luxurious hotels at convenient intervals for his night of rest. But we had the compensation in the charms of nature which go with the wilderness and wonders in all their primal glory.

When full day came over the hills, we cast a long admiring glance over the magnificent view and were borne reluctantly away to the Rodgers House in Virginia City. We roughly estimated that more than four hundred miles of travel in the park had been made on horseback.

MARGARET CRUIKSHANK

—◆—

*I*n 1883 the Northern Pacific finished building its transcontinental railroad and opened Yellowstone Park to a flood of middle-class tourists from all over America. One of them was Margaret Cruikshank, a fifty-eight-year-old schoolteacher from Minneapolis.

Unfortunately for Margaret, she arrived in August when three VIP parties were visiting the park—one led by U.S. president Chester A. Arthur, another by Northern Pacific president Henry Villard, and a third by Rufus Hatch of the Yellowstone Development Company. These dignitaries preempted hotel accommodations.

Cruikshank and the few other unaccompanied women were left to fend for themselves—and to seek help from Victorian gentlemen. Cruikshank enjoyed the natural wonders, but she was quick to condemn the tent hotels and crude log structures where she thought her hosts were serving horsemeat.

Miss Cruikshank's diary is in the Yellowstone National Park Research Library. An abridged version was published in Montana, The Magazine of Western History *in 1960. The version here is abridged further.*

AN UNESCORTED LADY
ON TOUR—1883

From the diary of Margaret Cruikshank

The morning of August 23rd we left the Mammoth Hot Springs to make the round of the park. Our outfit was a light, strongly made two-seated vehicle, with an outside seat for the driver. It had a top and curtains all around that were kept rolled up for air and view. This vehicle was drawn by two strong horses, mountain-born and mountain-bred; for no other horseflesh could endure such toil for a day. Behind the carriage was a boot where were stored a small tent, blankets, and cooking utensils; oats and a bucket for the horses' use were not forgotten; while inside, under the seats, were boxes and baskets carrying provisions. Our wraps, waterproofs, handbags, and guidebooks also found places, and we were ready to start—four of us plus the driver.

What I have said about the horses will be appreciated when I state that the first thing was to climb Terrace Mountain. Within the distance of two miles, four "hitches" as they call them, carried us nearly 3,000 feet higher than the level of the hotel from which we started. At the steepest places we got out and walked—and then began our sufferings. The dirt was almost ankle deep and the heat and clarity of the air made it a serious business. Still it had to be done, if we expected those same horses to last through our journey. This may be laid down as certain: wherever you go there are streams to ford, corduroy to fall over, sagebrush plains to crawl along, and mountains to cross. The strong can stand it and enjoy it, but this is no place for the delicate. Even the strong would be satisfied with less of it. I never longed for railroads as I did there.

As we made our way to Norris, the first wonder was the Obsidian Cliffs, upheaved somewhat columnar masses of black volcanic glass suggesting mines of the finest anthracite. The road beneath them is macadamized with the fragments, a glass road a quarter of a mile long.

We had left the Hot Springs Hotel before eleven, and it was after dark when we reached Norris, so long are twenty-one miles in the Park. It had been hot during the day, but as evening approached we were glad to draw about us heavy wraps. This was our constant experience. It was well that accident had prevented our wearing the usually advertised winter clothing; in the middle of the day, especially when climbing hills, it would have been intolerable. Our faithful driver Isaac sometimes tried our patience by care for his horses, but we were satisfied afterwards that he was right; at the least we fared better than most.

As we started just in advance of the first detachment of the Hatch Party (some twenty-five—all that the slender accommodations could provide for at once), we had had the pleasure all day of being passed by equestrians and teams, and now as we mounted the slight hill on which the hotel tents were placed we found ourselves the last of a numerous party and no welcome addition. The caravanserai at Norris consisted of half a dozen tents: one for the dining room, one for kitchen, and four for sleeping; and all told, drivers included, there were seventy of us there that night.

The accommodations were ludicrously insufficient and all who could provide for themselves at once withdrew. Among these were our two fellow passengers, a gentleman and his wife. Guided by Isaac they found a tolerable camping place, ate a hastily cooked supper, set up their three yards of canvas and crawled in. "Miss A." and myself, however, had no tent, and relied upon the overtasked resources of Norris. But where did all the seventy come from? There were many parties in the park and they all focused that night at Norris. It had been the plan of the park authorities that the best accommodations should be reserved for the Hatch party, but a high "military dignitary" had stolen a march upon them, gotten there first and had taken possession of at least one tent for the accommodation of his ladies. When therefore the Hatch party arrived great was their dissatisfaction to find even the poor accommodations that had been promised them not at their command.

"How and where shall I sleep?" became the important question. Miss A. and I at once resigned all hope of decent accommodation, thankful if only we were not left utterly shelterless. There fortune favored us and we found a most agreeable fellow sufferer in an English lady, a Miss Neave. She was one of those independent single women of wealth and position determined to see foreign countries. With her own servants she had been camping in the park for a month. She had pitched her tents or "broken camp" as fancy dictated, staying till fully satisfied in favored spots. How we envied her! It is the only true way to see the park.

We three "lone women" made common cause, and the host of the "grand hotel," as soon as supper was cleared away, informed us that he would give us a corner of the dining tent, but he had no other accommodation to offer. In this same tent fifteen gentlemen were to sleep. They were busy arranging their blankets when we went in. Some had two, and indulged in the luxury of a blanket beneath as well as above them. Handbags in hand and each with her blanket, we marched to our appointed corner. The host (poor driven man) was graciousness itself. "Ladies, if you have any pins I will put up a curtain for you." The pins were provided, but the curtain, a dirty piece of burlap, was "as odd as Dick's hatband" (that went half-way round and tucked under). It left the broad side wholly exposed. "Here, ladies, is a pillow for you," and with these encouraging words he hauled out from beneath a crude bench (where it had been partly on the bare ground and partly on a quarter of beef) a very dirty burlap sack full, he said, of potatoes! After these princely acts of hospitality he left us to our slumbers.

August 24—Having got through the night the next thing was how to make a toilet. Alas! no conventionalities, no decencies for us that morning. I appealed to our English friend, Miss Neave. "Shake yourself like a donkey—that is all you can do," said she, and as an old campaigner I felt that she knew.

Seeing no possible chance of even a tin basin to myself (no, not even a mug of water), I took courage and cloth in hand and advanced to the wash bench. "Will you please sir pour a little water over this cloth for me?" The nearest gentleman obliged me, with my wet cloth I rubbed off my face and fingertips, and my toilet was made. My hair was not touched from my rising of one day at the Hot Springs till my going to bed of the next at the Upper Geyser Basin! After such a night stimulants were much in demand. Miss A. and I had a mere vial of brandy, but we were glad enough to have recourse to it and offered some to Miss Neave. She declined, brandy not being her "tipple," but went off into the kitchen where she got hot water and condensed milk and came back with a whiskey punch, which she kindly shared with us. There was no getting through such an experience without frequent "little goes" of strong waters. One English lady of the Hatch party came up to Miss Neave and seemed solicitous of a closer acquaintance with her. Miss N. was polite but cool, and when said lady retired remarked to us, "That person is of what we call the tradesman class in England." Wasn't that English? But Miss Neave was right—the English of the Hatch Party were certainly not highbred.

The Norris Geyser Basin is on the headwaters of the Gibbon River, one of the branches of the Madison. From the road we survey it, a square mile or so of hot springs and geyser-like action. We look down upon a valley that seems all boiling water, mud puffs, embryo geysers, etc. just crusted over with a sheet of geyserite and looking exceedingly treacherous. They say explorers have ventured there, but I wouldn't for any money.

Our next stage was Marshall's on the forks of the Firehole River. To reach this we went through Gibbon Canyon, the rocks often towering above us but neither so narrow nor so dark as to be very impressive. In some places the rocks encroach so that the road is in the river, but only for a short distance. Wherever one goes in the park boiling springs may be found. There is one close to the Gibbon River, so close that it is difficult to get by it. A team that we met there had come to grief—at least one of the horses certainly had. The poor creature had fallen not into the springs mud but into a quagmire that the escaping hot waters had made in the road. I hope it did not find its involuntary bath very hot. At any rate it was a warning to us. Passengers got out and picked our way across while Isaac managed the safe navigation of his team. Another team more luckless was almost wrecked, and we had to help them right themselves. Often the road is so narrow that precautions have to be taken a mile ahead to prevent the meeting of teams where it would be impossible to pass.

We constantly met the most rustic of vehicles drawn by the roughest of farm animals and filled by the genuine sons and daughters of the soil. It was really strange to see how perfectly this class appreciates the wonders of the place and how glad they were to leave for a while their hard labor for the adventurous, the beautiful, and the sublime.

So we went on a rather monotonous day's journey till the early afternoon brought us to the Forks of Firehole—Marshall's. This time we only stop to lunch and bait the horses. Marshall is a man who, having no permit, has chosen to assume that he could keep such a house of entertainment, that the Park Improvement Company would be glad to let him stay. When only rough teamsters and hunters visited the park I suppose he gave satisfaction. But now the crowds that throng there are of a more fastidious sort Marshall won't do. Marshall must go. The effective force here was only three—Marshall, his wife, and a Chinaman—and they are all overworked and all cross. Not being forethoughted or forehanded as to providing and not having very high standards I cannot praise their results.

A detachment of the Hatch Party had preceded us and eaten up everything lean, except some dry imported baker's bread and some poor cake. After a wearisome delay we managed to get some not very hot water with which we made some "Lieby's Extract" beef tea from our own stores. As we crumbled the baker's bread into this we were charged fifty cents apiece. We left as soon as possible.

The first thing that informed us that we were nearing our destination was a geyser in full blast. It was close to the river just where we had to cross it by a bridge (as you may imagine, boiling water is not good for horses' feet). It was the Riverside Geyser firing away across the river at an angle. If the wind sets directly towards the bridge there is no getting over till the performance is ended—ten to thirteen minutes. It goes off three times a day.

After this, every step revealed new wonders. The formations of world-renowned geysers—the Giant, the Castle, the Grotto—were around us, but I am sorry to say they were not in active operations, only spurting a little water in sprays, or throwing up an inconsiderable amount of steam. The sun was disappearing when we found ourselves before the semi-circle of tents—between twenty and thirty that formed the company's hotel. Back, hidden from ours by a tongue of pines, was the president's encampment.

The hotel manager came forward cordially and, after a few moments of puzzled thought, took us to a tent that was to be all our own. I could but exclaim (after our experience at Norris), "Palatial magnificence!" We were put in complete possession of a thirteen-by-sixteen-foot tent with a rough-hewn wooden door fastened by a button inside and with a string to wind round a nail outside, when ladies were "not at home." It had a bright-striped hemp carpet tacked all round to the lowest bar of its frame and a good mattress bed on the floor with a white honeycomb quilt. The washstand was a rough packing box, but it was furnished with a pitcher and basin, plenty of soft geyser water, soap, and two towels.

We heard a "Swooop!" and "There he goes!" It was dear Old Faithful—the never disappointing, the beautiful, the grand, the typical geyser. Mr. Hobart drew aside the tent curtain and there, not an eighth of a mile away, towered in the rosy evening light the clean shaft, the fearless column. For a while we could only look and exclaim; the display lasted some five or six minutes. There are others, geysers that rise higher, much, but for all practical purposes this is enough; and as you start back in dread and awe, the 130 or 140 feet is just as grand as if it were 200 or more. Then Faithful rises so straight and clean, uninterfered with by side spurts and splashings, that he is really the perfect geyser. Bless him! He is so entirely all that we had anticipated and was so reliable, playing for us every hour, that we learned to love him.

In my guidebook I read that the little pools around Old Faithful have "pink and yellow margins and being constantly wet the colors are 'beautiful beyond description'." Then all I can say is that I must be colorblind. I could see faint ashes—of rose tint, a pearly gray, and the tawny yellow of iron rust—but "brilliant beyond description" makes one imagine vivid greens, intense yellows, clear blues, flaming scarlets, and flowing crimsons; and I saw none of these.

After Old Faithful the most satisfactory sight was the Sawmill Geyser. It erupted several times during the two hours, from twenty to thirty minutes at a time, with a regular kind of throb that at a little distance sounds like a sawmill.

It kindly gave us one of its most beautiful exhibitions. It rises from a lovely blue pool. It throws up not a shaft but a full fountain not more than thirty feet. But the water is so beautifully broken into large drops that flash like diamonds in the sun that while the performance lasts it is impossible to turn away. Lingering about, in hopes of seeing the Grand, we saw the Sawmill twice.

Early in the afternoon we were obliged to leave and journey back to Marshall's. We had a tolerably good supper, which I enjoyed. Part of the reason was that our party got in early and the overworked cook was not so rushed. We had fish nicely fried and quite tolerable coffee. I often found it difficult when things were at their worst to force down enough to sustain nature, such abominable messes were served up to us.

Above the square part of the building was a great loft, and this was elegantly subdivided into cells by burlap partitions reaching rather more than halfway up. Judging by their size there must have been more than a dozen of these little cubbyholes. Into these most of us were stowed.

Our room was in the southeast corner upstairs and had two beds in it, one at each end. Mrs. Gobeen was our roommate. It fell to my lot to sleep where the eaves came down over me like the crust over the blackbird in the pie. Mrs. Gobeen objected to having the window open. The bed was stuffed with sagebrush and had a horrid medicinal, quininey smell. And though the bedclothes may have been clean, I fancied that they had covered every teamster in the valley, besides being washed in that hot spring till the blankets were perfect felt. Moreover, with the sagacity usually exhibited by the lower classes in bed making, every double blanket had its fold up towards the head, so that if you were too warm you had to throw off both thicknesses or neither.

It was the morning of Monday, August 27, that we were to leave Marshall's for the falls, striking off in a northeasterly direction from the north and south course. How long it seemed before we could get Isaac started! Our fresh team went off at a round pace, the little black mule doing particularly good service. Our serenity was restored and we gave ourselves up to such enjoyment as we could get out of our long hot dusty ride. What a view! Here and there, near and far, clouds of steam rising through the dark pines told of concealed wonders never to be enjoyed by us, while all around rose the mountains. It was at noon camp in Hayden Valley that we gathered fir cones and made fire to boil our coffee and cook our eggs. Strange, what a flavor there is to such simple experiences. I shall always love the spot even though I will never see it again.

Somewhere on this route Isaac pointed to the turning that led to Yellowstone Lake—only fourteen miles off and we could not go! It made us heartsick. We had neither the time nor the money it would have required, nor were there any public accommodations there.

Tuesday, August 28—The sun was not as high as it should have been to show the Lower Falls to the best advantage, but it was enough. It was all perfectly wild and untouched nature and grandeur unsurpassed.

Niagara is the standard by which all cataracts are judged. Well, this was not Niagara with its immensity of volume and power, but the general feeling was that in everything else the Lower Fall was greatly the superior. The setting was so superb—the dark green of the pines, the emerald green of the water, the white foam of the broken masses, and the wonderful, wonderful canyon. Then from the fall, the river dashed wildly away, like a hurt thing and down, down in the bottom of the canyon it looked so frenzied that it no longer seemed merely water. We looked at it from a height of 1,875 feet sheer depth! But the Falls and the Canyon! How could we turn away and leave them after such a mere glimpse? The sun every instant shone more directly into the canyon, fairly illuminating it. We all agreed that earth could not furnish another such beautiful sight. I shall never forget it. How thankful I am to Miss Abbott for getting me there! I think we stood on the very spot from which my very best stereographs were taken.

We had to go; for we had to reach Marshall's again that night. By eleven o'clock we had set out on our return journey. There were a few objects of interest that in our haste the evening before we had left unvisited. We stopped for a short time at Sulphur Mountain, apparently a mass of sulphur enclosed in a thin shell of geyserite.

Wednesday, August 29—We had no geyserial premonitions that night at Marshall's to disturb our slumbers, and we were getting used to quininey mattresses and smelly felted blankets. We slept well, but early rising is a natural concomitant of the park air and excitement. I believe we had horse meat for breakfast and everything was poorly cooked. We were very willing to see the last of that place.

Fifteen miles brought us to Norris, where under the trees we took our last lunch. About one o'clock we resumed our journey. This last stage was tiresome in the extreme. It promised nothing to break the monotony.

We were within the last five miles of Mammoth when we entered upon the descent of Terrace Mountain. A cloud that had added to the beauties of sunset suddenly grew threatening. It rapidly spread over the sky and rain began to fall. It was now quite dark, and how cheery the bright lights of the hotel looked! Oh! At last! We were there! At the sound of our wheels, various officials rushed out with umbrellas to assist us to dismount and to help us up the rather ladder-like steps of the grand entrance, for all who have made the tour of the park are expected to return half dead, spent, and powerless.

ERNEST THOMPSON SETON

—◊—

In 1886 the army took over administration of Yellowstone National Park and began enforcing a no guns policy. Soon animals that had fled from public view to avoid slaughter reappeared where tourists could see them. When luxury hotels began dumping garbage in nearby forests, bear watching became as popular with tourists as viewing geysers. One tourist who went to the park to watch bears was the famous wildlife artist, naturalist, and writer Ernest Thompson Seton.

Seton, who helped found the Boy Scouts of America, not only wrote the first Boy Scout Handbook, he also wrote and illustrated popular stories about wild animals for magazines and books. Nearly every boy and girl in America knew about Seton and his stories.

In 1897 he came to Yellowstone Park to do an inventory of large animals for a magazine that focused on wildlife conservation. On that trip Seton saw a fight between a grizzly and a momma black bear protecting her invalid cub that everybody called "Johnny." Seton's story about the fight became the basis for his most famous story, "Johnny Bear." Seton was so fond of the story that he told it a second time from the perspective of Wahb, the subject of his book Biography of a Grizzly.

"Johnny Bear" originally appeared in Scribner's Magazine and was republished in Seton's book Wild Animals I Have Known. The following is a condensed version.

JOHNNY BEAR—1897

From Ernest Thompson Seton's book
Wild Animals I Have Known

Johnny was a queer little bear cub that lived with Grumpy, his mother, in Yellowstone Park. They were among the many bears that found a desirable home in the country about the Fountain Hotel.

The steward of the hotel had ordered the kitchen garbage to be dumped in an open glade of the surrounding forest, thus providing, throughout the season, a daily feast for the bears, and their numbers have increased each year since the law of the land has made the park a haven of refuge where no wild thing may be harmed. They have accepted man's peace offering, and many of them have become so well known to the hotel men that they have received names suggested by their looks or ways. Slim Jim was a very long-legged thin black bear; Snuffy was a black bear that looked as though he had been singed; Fatty was a very fat, lazy bear that always lay down to eat; the Twins were two half-grown, ragged specimens that always came and went together. But Grumpy and Little Johnny were the best known of them all.

Grumpy was the biggest and fiercest of the black bears, and Johnny, apparently her only son, was a peculiarly tiresome little cub for he seemed never to cease either grumbling or whining. This probably meant that he was sick, for a healthy little bear does not grumble all the time, any more than a healthy child. And indeed Johnny looked sick;

After large hotels began dumping their garbage in nearby forests, bear watching became as popular as viewing geysers and falls.
National Park Service photo by J. P. Clum, 1910

he was the most miserable specimen in the park. His whole appearance suggested dyspepsia; and this I quite understood when I saw the awful mixtures he would eat at the garbage heap. Anything at all that he fancied he would try. And his mother allowed him to do as he pleased; so, after all, it was chiefly her fault, for she should not have permitted such things.

Johnny had only three good legs, his coat was faded and mangy, his limbs were thin, and his ears and paunch were disproportionately large. Yet his mother thought the world of him. She was evidently convinced that he was a little beauty and the Prince of all Bears, so, of course, she quite spoiled him. She was always ready to get into trouble on his account, and he was always delighted to lead her there.

Although such a wretched little failure, Johnny was far from being a fool, for he usually knew just what he wanted and how to get it, if teasing his mother could carry the point.

It was in the summer of 1897 that I made their acquaintance. I was in the park to study the home life of the animals and had been told that in the woods near the Fountain Hotel I could see bears at any time, which, of course, I scarcely believed.

Early the next morning I went to this bears' banqueting hall in the pines and hid in the nearest bushes. All morning the bears came and went or wandered near my hiding place without discovering me; and, except for one or two brief quarrels, there was nothing very exciting to note. But about three in the afternoon it became more lively.

There were then four large bears feeding on the heap. In the middle was Fatty, sprawling at full length as he feasted, a picture of placid ursine content, puffing just a little at times as he strove to save himself the trouble of moving by darting out his tongue like a long red serpent, farther and farther, in quest of the tidbits just beyond claw reach.

Behind him Slim Jim was puzzling over the anatomy and attributes of an ancient lobster. It was something outside his experience, but the principle, "In case of doubt take the trick," is well known in bear land and settled the difficulty.

The other two were clearing out fruit tins with marvelous dexterity. One supple paw would hold the tin while the long tongue would dart again and again through the narrow opening, avoiding the sharp edges, yet cleaning out the can to the last taste of its sweetness.

This pastoral scene lasted long enough to be sketched, but was ended abruptly. My eye caught a movement on the hilltop whence all the bears had come, and out stalked a very large black bear with a tiny cub. It was Grumpy and Little Johnny.

The old bear stalked down the slope toward the feast, and Johnny hitched alongside, grumbling as he came, his mother watching him as solicitously as ever a hen did her single chick. When they were within thirty yards of the garbage heap, Grumpy turned to her son and said something which, judging from its effect, must have meant, "Johnny, my child, I think you had better stay here while I go and chase those fellows away."

Johnny obediently waited; but he wanted to see, so he sat up on his hind legs with eyes agog and ears acock.

Grumpy came striding along with dignity, uttering warning growls as she approached the four bears. They were too much engrossed to pay any heed to the fact that yet another one of them was coming, till Grumpy, now within fifteen feet, let out a succession of loud coughing sounds, and charged into them. Strange to say, they did not pretend to face her, but as soon as they saw who it was, scattered and all fled for the woods. Slim Jim could safely trust his heels, and the others were not far behind. But poor Fatty, puffing hard and waddling like any other very fat creature, got along but slowly. Unluckily for him, he fled in the direction of Johnny, so that Grumpy overtook him in a few bounds and gave him a couple of sound slaps in the rear which, if they did not accelerate his pace, at least made him bawl, and saved him by changing his direction. Grumpy, now left alone in possession of the feast, turned toward her son and uttered the whining Er-r-r Er-r-r Er-r-r-r. Johnny responded eagerly. He came hoppity-hop on his three good legs as fast as he could, and, joining her on the garbage, they began to have such a good time that Johnny actually ceased grumbling.

He had evidently been there before now, for he seemed to know quite well the staple kinds of canned goods. One might almost have supposed that he had learned the brands, for a lobster tin had no charm for him as long as he could find those that once were filled with jam. Some of the tins gave him much trouble, as he was too greedy or too clumsy to escape being scratched by the sharp edges. One seductive fruit tin had a hole so large that he found he could force his head into it, and for a few minutes his joy was full as he licked into all the farthest corners. But when he tried to draw his head out, his sorrows began, for he found himself caught. He could not get out, and he scratched and screamed like any other spoiled child, giving his mother no end of concern, although she seemed not to know how to help him. When at length he got the tin off his head, he revenged himself by hammering it with his paws till it was perfectly flat.

A large syrup can made him happy for a long time. It had a lid, so that the hole was round and smooth; but it was not big enough to admit his head, and he could not touch its riches with his tongue stretched out its longest. He soon hit on a plan, however. Putting in his little black arm, he churned it around, then drew out and licked it clean; and while he licked one he got the other one ready; and he did this again and again, until the can was as clean inside as when first it had left the factory.

A broken mousetrap seemed to puzzle him. He clutched it between his fore paws and held it firmly for study. The cheesy smell about it was decidedly good, but the thing responded in such an uncanny way, when he slapped it, that he kept back a cry for help only by the exercise of unusual self-control. After gravely inspecting it, with his head first on this side and then on that, and his lips puckered into a little tube, he submitted it to the same punishment as that meted out to the refractory fruit tin, and was rewarded by discovering a nice little bit of cheese in the very heart of the culprit.

Johnny had evidently never heard of ptomaine poisoning, for nothing came amiss. After the jams and fruits gave out he turned his attention to the lobster and sardine cans, and was not appalled by even the army beef. His paunch grew quite balloon-like and from much licking his arms looked thin and shiny, as though he was wearing black silk gloves. It occurred to me that I might now be in a really dangerous place. For it is one thing surprising a bear that has no family responsibilities, and another stirring up a bad-tempered old mother by frightening her cub.

"Supposing," I thought, "that cranky Little Johnny should wander over to this end of the garbage and find me in the hole; he will at once set up a squall, and his mother, of course, will think I am hurting him, and, without giving me a chance to explain, may forget the rules of the park and make things very unpleasant."

Luckily, all the jam pots were at Johnny's end; he stayed by them, and Grumpy stayed by him. At length he noticed that his mother had a better tin than any he could find, and, as he ran whining to take it from her, he chanced to glance away up the slope. There he saw something that made him sit up and utter a curious little Koff Koff Koff Koff Koff.

His mother turned quickly, and sat up to see "what the child was looking at." I followed their gaze, and there, oh horrors! was an enormous grizzly bear. He was a monster; he looked like a fur-clad omnibus coming through the trees.

Johnny set up a whine at once and got behind his mother. She uttered a deep growl, and all her back hair stood on end. Mine did too, but I kept as still as possible.

With stately tread the grizzly came on. His vast shoulders sliding along his sides, and his silvery robe swaying at each tread, like the trappings on an elephant, gave an impression of power that was appalling.

Johnny began to whine more loudly, and I fully sympathized with him now, though I did not join in. After a moment's hesitation Grumpy turned to her noisy cub and said something that sounded to me like two or three short coughs—Koff Koff Koff. But I imagine that she really said, "My child, I think you had better get up that tree, while I go and drive the brute away."

At any rate, that was what Johnny did, and this what she set out to do. But Johnny had no notion of missing any fun. He wanted to see what was going to happen. So he did not rest contented where he was hidden in the thick branches of the pine, but combined safety with view by climbing to the top-most branch that would bear him, and there, sharp against the sky, he squirmed about and squealed aloud in his excitement. The branch was so small that it bent under his weight, swaying this way and that as he shifted about, and every moment I expected to see it snap off. If it had been broken when swaying my way, Johnny would certainly have fallen on me, and this would probably have resulted in bad feelings between myself and his mother; but the limb was tougher than it looked, or perhaps Johnny had had plenty of experience, for he neither lost his hold nor broke the branch.

Meanwhile, Grumpy stalked out to meet the grizzly. She stood as high as she could and set all her bristles on end; then, growling and chopping her teeth, she faced him.

The grizzly, so far as I could see, took no notice of her. He came striding toward the feast as though alone. But when Grumpy got within twelve feet of him she uttered a succession of short, coughy roars, and, charging, gave him a tremendous blow on the ear. The grizzly was surprised; but he replied with a left-hander that knocked her over like a sack of hay.

Nothing daunted, but doubly furious, she jumped up and rushed at him.

Then they clinched and rolled over and over, whacking and pounding, snorting and growling, and making no end of dust and rumpus. But above all their noise I could clearly hear Little Johnny, yelling at the top of his voice, and evidently encouraging his mother to go right in and finish the grizzly at once.

Why the grizzly did not break her in two I could not understand. After a few minutes' struggle, during which I could see nothing but dust and dim flying legs, the two separated as by mutual consent—perhaps the regulation time was up—and for a while they stood glaring at each other, Grumpy at least much winded.

The grizzly would have dropped the matter right there. He did not wish to fight. He had no idea of troubling himself about Johnny. All he wanted was a quiet meal. But no! The moment he took one step toward the garbage pile, that is, as Grumpy thought, toward Johnny, she went at him again. But this time the grizzly was ready for her. With one blow he knocked her off her feet and sent her crashing on to a huge upturned pine root. She was fairly staggered this time. The force of the blow, and the rude reception of the rooty ant-lers, seemed to take all the fight out of her. She scrambled over and tried to escape. But the grizzly was mad now. He meant to punish her, and dashed around the root. For a min-ute they kept up a dodging chase about it; but Grumpy was quicker of foot, and somehow always managed to keep the root between herself and her foe, while Johnny, safe in the tree, continued to take an intense and uproarious interest.

At length, seeing he could not catch her that way, the grizzly sat up on his haunches; and while he doubtless was planning a new move, old Grumpy saw her chance, and mak-ing a dash, got away from the root and up to the top of the tree where Johnny was perched.

Johnny came down a little way to meet her, or perhaps so that the tree might not break off with the additional weight. Having photographed this interesting group from my hiding place, I thought I must get a closer picture at any price, and for the first time in the day's proceedings I jumped out of the hole and ran under the tree. This move proved a great mistake, for here the thick lower boughs came between, and I could see nothing at all of the bears at the top.

I was close to the trunk, and was peering about and seek-ing for a chance to use the camera, when old Grumpy began to come down, chopping her teeth and uttering her threaten-ing cough at me. While I stood in doubt, I heard a voice far behind me calling:

"Say, Mister! You better look out; that ole b'ar is liable to hurt you."

I turned to see the cowboy of the hotel on his horse. He had been riding after the cattle, and chanced to pass near just as events were moving quickly.

"Do you know these bears?" said I, as he rode up.

"Wall, I reckon I do," said he. "That there little one up top is Johnny; he's a little crank. An' the big un is Grumpy; she's a big crank. She's mighty onreliable gen'relly, but she's always strictly ugly when Johnny hollers like that."

"I should much like to get her picture when she comes down," said I.

"Tell ye what I'll do: I'll stay by on the pony, an' if she goes to bother you I reckon I can keep her off," said the man.

He accordingly stood by as Grumpy slowly came down from branch to branch, growling and threatening. But when she neared the ground she kept on the far side of the trunk and finally slipped down and ran into the woods, without the slightest pretense of carrying out any of her dreadful threats. Thus Johnny was again left alone. He climbed up to his old perch and resumed his monotonous whining:

Wah! Wah! Wah! ("Oh, dear! Oh, dear! Oh dear!")

I got the camera ready, and was arranging deliberately to take his picture in his favorite and peculiar attitude for threnodic song, when all at once he began craning his neck and yelling, as he had done during the fight.

I looked where his nose pointed, and here was the grizzly coming on straight toward me—not charging, out striding along, as though he meant to come the whole distance.

I said to my cowboy friend, "Do you know this bear?"

He replied, "Wall! I reckon I do. That's the ole grizzly. He's the biggest b'ar in the park. He gen'relly minds his own business, but he ain't scared o' nothin'; an' today, ye see, he's been scrappin' so he's liable to be ugly."

"I would like to take his picture," said I, "and if you will help me, I am willing to take some chances on it."

"All right," said he, with a grin. "I'll stand by on the horse, an' if he charges you I'll charge him; an' I kin knock him down once, but I can't do it twice. You better have your tree picked out."

As there was only one tree to pick out, and that was the one that Johnny was in, the prospect was not alluring. I imagined myself scrambling up there next to Johnny, and then Johnny's mother coming up after me, with the grizzly below to catch me when Grumpy should throw me down.

The grizzly came on, and I snapped him at forty yards, then again at twenty yards; and still he came quietly toward me. I sat down on the garbage and made ready. Eighteen yards, sixteen yards, twelve yards, eight yards, and still he came, while the pitch of Johnny's protests kept rising proportionately. Finally at five yards he stopped, and swung his huge bearded head to one side, to see what was making the aggravating row in the treetop, giving me a profile view, and I snapped the camera. At the click he turned on me with a thunderous G-R-O-W-L! and I sat still and trembling, wondering if my last moment had come. For a second he glared at me, and I could note that little green electric lamp in each of his eyes. Then he slowly turned and picked up a large tomato can.

"Goodness!" I thought, "is he going to throw that at me?" But he deliberately licked it out, dropped it, and took another, paying thenceforth no heed whatever either to me or to Johnny, evidently considering us equally beneath his notice.

I backed slowly and respectfully out of his royal presence, leaving him in possession of the garbage, while Johnny kept on caterwauling from his safety perch.

What became of Grumpy the rest of that day I do not know. Johnny, after bewailing for a time, realized that there was no sympathetic hearer of his cries, and therefore very sagaciously stopped them. Having no mother now to plan for him, he began to plan for himself, and at once proved that he was better stuff than he seemed. After watching, with a look of profound cunning on his little black face, and waiting till the grizzly was some distance away, he silently slipped down behind the trunk, and, despite his three-leggedness, ran like a hare to the next tree, never stopping to breathe till he was on its topmost bough. For he was thoroughly convinced that the only object that the grizzly had in life was to kill him, and he seemed quite aware that his enemy could not climb a tree.

Another long and safe survey of the grizzly, who really paid no heed to him whatever, was followed by another dash for the next tree, varied occasionally by a cunning feint to mislead the foe. So he went dashing from tree to tree and climbing each to its very top, although it might be but ten feet from the last, till he disappeared in the woods. After, perhaps, ten minutes, his voice again came floating on the breeze, the habitual querulous whining which told me he had found his mother and had resumed his customary appeal to her sympathy.

The last time I saw Johnny he was in the top of a tree, bewailing his unhappy lot as usual while his mother was dashing about among the pines, "with a chip on her shoulder," seeking for someone—anyone—that she could punish for Johnny's sake, provided, of course, that it was not a big grizzly.

This was early in August, but there were not lacking symptoms of change in old Grumpy. She was always reckoned "onsartain," and her devotion to Johnny seemed subject to her characteristic. This perhaps accounted for the fact that when the end of the month was near, Johnny would sometimes spend half a day in the top of some tree, alone, miserable, and utterly unheeded.

The last chapter of his history came to pass after I had left the region. One day at grey dawn he was tagging along behind his mother as she prowled in the rear of the hotel. A newly hired Irish girl was already astir in the kitchen. On looking out, she saw, as she thought, a calf where it should not be, and ran to shoo it away. That open kitchen door held unmeasured terrors for Grumpy, and she ran in such alarm that Johnny caught the infection, and not being able to keep up with her, he made for the nearest tree, which unfortunately turned out to be a post, and soon, too soon, he arrived at its top, some seven feet from the ground, and there poured forth his woes on the chilly morning air, while Grumpy apparently felt justified in continuing her flight alone. When the girl came near and saw that she had treed some wild animal, she was as much frightened as her victim. But others of the kitchen staff appeared, and recognizing the vociferous Johnny, they decided to make him a prisoner.

A collar and chain were brought, and after a struggle, during which several of the men got well scratched, the collar was buckled on Johnny's neck and the chain made fast to the post.

When he found that he was held, Johnny was simply too mad to scream. He bit and scratched and tore till he was tired out. Then he lifted up his voice again to call his mother. She did appear once or twice in the distance, but could not make up her mind and so disappeared. And Johnny was left to his fate.

He put in most of that day in alternate struggling and crying. Toward evening he was worn out, and glad to accept the meal that was brought by Norah, who felt herself called on to play mother, since she had chased his own mother away.

When night came it was very cold; but Johnny nearly froze at the top of the post before he would come down and accept the warm bed provided at the bottom. During the day that followed, Grumpy came often to the garbage heap, but soon apparently succeeded in forgetting all about her son. He was daily tended by Norah, and received all his meals from her. He also received something else; for one day he scratched her when she brought his food, and she very properly spanked him till he squealed. For a few hours he sulked; he was not used to such treatment. But hunger subdued him and thenceforth he held his new guardian in wholesome respect. She, too, began to take an interest in the poor motherless little wretch, and within a fortnight Johnny showed signs of developing a new character. He was much less noisy. He still expressed his hunger in a whining Er-r-r Er-r-r Er-r-r, but he rarely squealed now, and his unruly outbursts entirely ceased.

By the third week of September the change was still more marked. Utterly abandoned by his own mother, all his interest had centered in Norah, and she had fed and spanked him into an exceedingly well-behaved little bear. Sometimes she would allow him a taste of freedom, and he then showed his bias by making, not for the woods, but for the kitchen where she was, and following her around on his hind legs.

As the hotel was to be closed in October, there was talk of turning Johnny loose or of sending him to the Washington Zoo, but Norah had claims that she would not forego.

When the frosty nights of late September came, Johnny had greatly improved in his manners, but he had also developed a bad cough. An examination of his lame leg had shown that the weakness was not in the foot, but much more deeply seated, perhaps in the hip, and that meant a feeble and tottering constitution.

He did not get fat, as do most bears in fall; indeed, he continued to fail. His little round belly shrank in, his cough became worse, and one morning he was found very sick and shivering in his bed by the post. Norah brought him indoors, where the warmth helped him so much that thenceforth he lived in the kitchen.

For a few days he seemed better, and his old-time pleasure in seeing things revived. The great blazing fire in the range particularly appealed to him and made him sit up in his old attitude when the opening of the door brought the wonder to view. After a week he lost interest even in that and drooped more and more each day. Finally not the most exciting noises or scenes around him could stir up his old fondness for seeing what was going on.

He coughed a good deal, too, and seemed wretched, except when in Norah's lap. Here he would cuddle up contentedly, and whine most miserably when she had to set him down again in his basket.

A few days before the closing of the hotel, he refused his usual breakfast, and whined softly till Norah took him in her lap; then he feebly snuggled up to her, and his soft Er-r-r Er-r-r grew fainter, till it ceased. Half an hour later, when she laid him down to go about her work, Little Johnny had lost the last trace of his anxiety to see and know what was going on.

ELEANOR CORTHELL

—⟋⟍—

Eleanor Corthell's husband "could only fizz and fume" when she announced in 1903 that she was taking their seven children to Yellowstone National Park by team and wagon. But he could think of no good reason to stop her. By then the park had been transformed into a civilized park where an unaccompanied woman could travel without fear of being attacked by Indians or bears. The Army Corps of Engineers, under the direction of Captain Hiram Chittenden, had completed a network of roads in the park that were among the best in the United States, certainly good enough to be navigated by Mrs. Corthell's sixteen-year-old son. There were stores where the Corthells could buy supplies and post offices where they could keep in contact with family and friends.

Although the park had several grand hotels, the Corthells camped out for their entire two-month adventure. This meant that Mrs. Corthell had to manage not only the logistics of the trip but also cooking and laundry—all out of doors. That might sound like an enormous challenge, but as Eleanor would have pointed out, she would have been in charge of all those duties had she stayed at home.

Despite the relative tranquility of Yellowstone Park at the time, the Corthells had plenty of adventures. Their travels across the ranch country of central Wyoming reminded them of Owen Wister's novel **The Virginian**, which many consider to be the first Western. In the park they kept their eyes out for *black bear cubs like Johnny Bear and a grizzly like Wahb, who were the subjects of famous stories by the hugely popular naturalist and writer Ernest Thompson Seton.*

Eleanor's husband, Nellis, joined his family in the park and promptly ran afoul of regulations that were enforced by the army, which ran the park then. But Nellis was a prominent Wyoming attorney and he managed to talk himself down to a two-dollar fine.

Eleanor's story of her family trek was published in June 1905 in the magazine Independent. *She published an extended version in a self-published book,* A Family Trek to the Yellowstone, *in 1928. The following narrative draws from both versions.*

A FAMILY TREK TO YELLOWSTONE—1903

From a story and book by Mrs. N. E. Corthell

Nearly half a lifetime I have lived in Laramie, with all the while a great longing to see the wonders of the Yellowstone in season, out of season, when the house was full of babies, even when it was full of measles. As the older children outgrew marbles and dolls, I conceived the bold idea of stowing them all in a prairie schooner and sailing away over the Rocky Mountains, deserts, forests, and fords to the enchanted land five hundred miles away.

My husband offered strenuous objection of course to the crazy project, but could only fizz and fume and furnish the wherewithal, for the reasons advanced he found irresistible; such an ideal vacation for the children—a summer out-of-doors, seeing their native state! A chance for their geography, botany, zoology to be naturalized. To be drivers and cooks would put them on their own resources somewhat, a valuable education in itself. So economical, too! Such a fine opportunity for stretching of legs and lungs, with the park at the end! Reasons to turn a man's head, you see, so when the boys wrote along the wagon top "Park or Bust" that settled it, and we started July 4th, 1903.

I had resolved to "go light." A two-seated spring wagon, tent, stove, bedding, clothing, two weeks' provisions, besides my live freight, made up the load behind a pair of big road horses.

Yellowstone Park's excellent road system encouraged families to load the wagons with camping gear. Often they traveled hundreds of miles and camped out for weeks.
Pioneer Museum of Bozeman photo

The first day out was glorious. We drove thirty-three miles to the steel bridge down the Laramie River. The bracing air, fresh from Snowy Range, the changing scene, the fragrance of prairie flowers and wild sage, the blue of lupine and larkspur giving the effect of lakes here and there, the peaceful herds in grass knee deep, created a charm which we accepted as a good omen of the unknown before us.

We camped without tent or stove that night, for the small boys were "heap big Injuns," who scorned civilized ways. They whooped along on the warpath, examined old trails, read the sky, sent the "stinging fatal arrow" after rabbits, clamored for pioneer tales, then rolled up in blankets around the camp fire with only the stars overhead.

During the night we had an amusing experience to scare a tenderfoot blue. Sometime after midnight when the moon rose, I awoke, amazed to see a hundred head of range cattle lined up around us in a semi-circle, still as mice, their great eyes bulging with curiosity. I called to the boys, several heads bobbed up, and away the cattle scampered, only to return again and again in wild-eyed astonishment until their curiosity was sated, when they grazed off. After that I tried to sleep with one eye open. It can't be done out camping. Why does the morning sun inspire one with the fine courage lacking in the pale moonlight? Now I'm brave enough to "shoo" a whole herd of Texas steers or to grapple with all the dragons kind friends conjured for me—treacherous fords, snakes, bad lands—all of them, each and every.

You are wondering how eight people can be comfortable in two seats? That's easy. We piled our bedding fore, aft and amidships, with clothing in pillowslips, and so had seats for all, even choice ones. If you were a small boy, for instance, you could sit on a roll of bedding or sack of grain, hang your bare feet over the dashboard and hold the whip, if very good, the lines, or you could perch behind ready to hop off to chase a rabbit, or curl up on a soft pile, lay your head in mother's lap and sleep away the drowsy afternoon.

To the bridge there is one road only; beyond the bridge there are a dozen. Which one led to Little Medicine Crossing, our most direct route to Shirley Basin? We didn't know, and couldn't find out for one may travel a whole day beyond the bridge and not meet a soul, so we took the wrong road and had to make a dry camp at Como, reaching Medicine Bow the third day at noon. From here we drove north among the Freezeout Hills, through which the Virginian piloted Owen

Wister on his way to the Goose Egg Ranch. We arrived at the old Trading place about four o'clock. This is one of the famed historic spots in Wyoming, and many thrilling events have occurred here, but now it is abandoned, save that it is occupied by three young freighters passing through.

They courteously offered to camp outside and give us the house, but we were afraid of strangers, so after a hasty supper moved on ten miles and spread our tarpaulins on the bare plain.

Arriving at my friend Kirk Dyer's the next morning I told him of my foolish fears that the young men having their horses might have designs on ours. He rebuked me sternly and read me such a lecture as I shall never forget.

"Country people are honest," said he, "and you must take it for granted you are safer here than in Laramie and you get a square deal everywhere. Trust people and don't be that suspicious."

Such a happy day the children spent riding horseback eating Mrs. Dyer's cream biscuits.

Adjoining this ranch are the fossil fields of the Freezeout Hills in which two university boys were working. I would have taken them for young Comanches from their yells at the sight of home folks.

Next day was different. We were driving gaily along through the Quealy Meadow, where suddenly the wagon sank in the mire. While the horses struggled to pull it out, the king bolt snapped, and off they walked with the front wheels. My driver boy quietly stepped over the dashboard and walked off after them, still holding the lines.

For one despairing moment I thought the end of all things had come, when my wagon parted in the middle.

Noticing my forlorn face, one youngster thought it was time to laugh and exclaimed, "Gee, Mamma! This isn't exciting. The horses should have run away and smashed a few kids." Seeing how much worse things might have been I thanked my lucky stars and took heart again.

Shirley Basin proved to be the land of the Good Samaritan where every ranchman is your friend and neighbor, who pulls you out of the mud, mends your king bolts, agrees with you in politics, praises your husband, and treats you to ice cream in the evening, so the accident makes pleasant memory.

Now I must tell my troubles. We had started first on the third of July, run into a snowstorm and returned. But it was clear and warm and bright the next morning, and in our haste to be off we left the pocketbook in my desk. Imagine my predicament—a mother totally unused to business or cares outside her own domain, one hundred and fifty miles from home, with seven children and two horses to provide for, and not a cent of money!

We discovered our loss a few miles out from Laramie, but just then met friends driving in, who promised to have the pocketbook forwarded; and we went serenely on our way into this dilemma. We were put to our wits end to get oats, as yet our only necessity. The driver suggested that we trade off a hammock; my Daughter thought we could better spare bacon. It being a hot day, little Tad generously offered his overcoat as a basis of trade. The driver and I went to the store, each trying to brace the other. One was to mention bacon, that failing, the other to try hammock. Oh, I know exactly how a tramp feels when he begins asking for cold bites. At the first question, "Have you oats?" we received a "no" almost with relief, for now we needn't show our hands here.

We walked over to a ranchman's house, nerved up to try a bargain, until we saw the man, and the fine style in which he lived. Then we realized it would be like asking the president to swap a sack of oats for a side of bacon. No, we must put dignity into our need, so quaking like two criminals, I asked Mr. Blank for oats and "to send the bill to my husband, please." A fleeting, quizzical flutter of his eyelid brought out the wretched blunder of the pocketbook.

"But, my dear Madam," said he, "you must not be traveling with all those children to care for and no money." Then he brought from his desk a generous sum, saying, "Your husband can send me his check when convenient." My troubles were over, but was ever a deed more chivalrous "in day of old when knights were bold"?

In the Platte we toiled up the endless hills through deep sand. Sometimes it would be so sidling we would take turns with the spade and literally build a stretch of road. Sometimes we would all help push the wagon up a steep pitch. When the smaller children grew very tired from climbing, they took turns driving. The next older ones I partly carried, partly coaxed, until finally we were all up the last cruel hill. We suffered severely from thirst, for the water jug had bumped out and broken coming down a rough canyon. Suddenly someone said "tomatoes." Away down beneath the bedding we found them, cool and just to our taste, one quart can, two, then a third. And as Stewart White said of the cool breeze under a fallen tree, "Never have dinners or wines or men or women or talks of books or scenery or sport or the daintiest refinements of man's inventions given me half the luxury I enjoyed from that cup of tomato." To quote him further, "Real luxury cannot be bought, it must be worked for."

But climbing sandy hills is really not trouble when one is desperate for oats. Still it brought home vividly the suffering of the forty-niners, as the want of the pocketbook made me feel the shame of the penniless tramp.

The children are eagerly interested in everything they see, hear, or can catch. Tad announces that we have seen eight horned toads, caught five, and mailed three to the chum at home.

I wonder, where is the medicine that was in those boxes? Well if they spill the tablets they will have to drink sage tea when ill. Marvelous cures of many kinds in bitter sage.

Everybody is growing handy, even expert, in camp work. The boys can skin a cottontail or dress a sage hen equal to Kit Carson himself, while Daughter prepares a savory dinner or packs a mess box good enough for an army general.

The immensity of Wyoming begins to dawn on them. They hunt, swim, explore, and so learn to enjoy the special individual flavor of each locality. But all grow tired of the limitless sage—one million acres after another. Why do these vast, treeless plains bear one species of wood only and that so abundantly? When all the coal beds are empty and all the oil wells are dry, Wyoming sagebrush may be relied upon to warm and light the world. It makes an ideal campfire and bakes biscuits perfectly.

We are now over two hundred miles from home and approaching the Beaver Hill dragon. We have heard so much about it, though, that we are braced for trouble. With a good steel brake and a seventy-five-foot picket rope fastened behind for the children to pull back on, and me boosting on the underside to help the wagon on the sidling places out of that steep windy comb, we arrived safely at the foot, though three stagecoaches had blown over in one day the week before.

We entered Lander on July 22nd, where we received our first letter and the pocketbook. The anxious one was impatiently waiting to telephone, so I was soon at that office, rejoicing to hear the dear familiar voice, even in "Hello." Then, "Are you coming home or going on?" "Going on, of course." A nervous little laugh came over the wire, then silence. A pole fell or a wire broke somewhere out on the endless plains, and our talk was over. Such hard luck! Still thankful just for the sound of my husband's voice, we hurried on.

The girls like to press curious plants in books. Apropos of books, I shudder to this day when I recall the difference between the reading planned for them and what they read. Very carefully I searched the shelves for a few choice volumes. One of Shakespeare's comedies. I would take plenty of time some rainy day to read it well, when they must like it— even the youngest; *Ethics of the Dust* went in, for I longed to have my dear daughter a follower of Ruskin, too. Besides it was such a little book. One of Dickens, Captain Chittenden's Yellowstone Park guide book, two or three recent *Outlooks,* a first year Latin in case a backward child wanted to study—of such was my collection. Well, the only book they opened was the *Headless Horseman,* which a chum handed the driver as we were starting. Up and down the line it went, over and over.

The responsibility and anxiety of the long trip are laying hold of me, till I'm nearly overwhelmed. Four hundred miles from home, and only one letter!

What may have happened in all these weeks? Suppose a child should sicken. There's a man at home who would never forgive me should one of them be lost. Will the horses hold out? The food? Already two spokes are broken and wrapped together with baling wire. My bold driver says we shall go on if we have to drive into the park with every spoke bound up with baling wire. And the dangers anticipated did add a certain zest. "Give Ma something to fret about and she's happy," observed our twelve-year-old philosopher.

Our problems narrowed to a question of food, with the Continental Divide looming in the distance. How to cook enough for all those hungry children, where bread could not be bought, and still get ahead fifteen or twenty miles a day? The capacity of my oven was two tins of twelve biscuits each. These I filled three times at night, when darkness overtook me. That made seventy-two biscuits, three apiece every meal, but the boys wanted six and that was the problem. We caught a few fish, but saw no game from Lander on. We had gooseberry pie, all we wanted, and fresh strawberry shortcake once. All grew tired of our staples—bacon, beans, corn, coffee, sardines, prunes, and coldwater biscuits. When the boys felt particularly cross and sarcastic they gloated aloud over the memory of Mrs. Dyer's cream biscuits. Yet it is only fair to add that keen appetites and inspiring scenery made the want of variety of food seem unimportant, even when the butter gave out.

Over the Continental Divide to Jackson Hole was a continual surprise—the road was so good, smooth, hard, well graded—thanks to Captain Chittenden. The plain just gradually lifted up from Lander Valley until it rested on the divide, two hundred miles away. The spurt that took us over the pass wasn't so gradual. But it is fine to climb a thousand feet and look about when you have mounted to ten thousand feet and gaze at the crest of the continent, the Atlantic slope behind, the Pacific slope spreading before you, range after range, with intervening valley, gorge, river, lake, with the Grand Teton gleaming over all in the distance—magnificent, inspiration—your soul is filled with exaltation.

I get the grandeur of it under stress. When they called to see the clouds lift from the brow of Mount Moran I was lining up smoking hot buttermilk pancakes. Later, as the sun shot his golden lances among the fleecy mass and the woods echoed the children's hallelujahs, I was up to my elbows in the washtub, making us spick and span for the park. So, with a little, sudsy shirt in my hand, I'd run to see earth and morning meet in a burst of glory on Teton heights.

We meet so many outfits returning, from Salt Lake, Idaho, Kansas, everywhere. Few have come so far as we, though we traveled two days with families from Jewell, Kansas, who before reaching home would have gone a thousand miles farther than we.

One of the men said he never had a vacation before and now he meant to have his fill. They intended to stay until the hunting season opened, to get big game.

Many of the returning outfits had great four-horse freight wagons, loaded with bedsprings, mattresses, chairs, tables, Easter bonnets, and a multitude of burdensome luxuries. "Burdensome," their careworn faces said plainly. Grateful we are to Stewart Edward White for his advice to "go light." And it is interesting to make one dish serve for six. By putting pillowcases inside of gunnysacks we carried necessary clothing without much weight or waste of space. Grocery stores are never more than three days apart so why a mess wagon? We hauled just enough canned goods over the divide to last us to Moran, that is, Allen's ranch, where all good things were to be had, even butter.

I know one young man who made the trip in company with his mother, sister, sweetheart, and others, but no larger party than ours, yet he had a regular caravan, a four-horse mess wagon, phaeton, buggy, and horseman. We camped near them occasionally and saw how every night he had to be responsible for a dozen horses, see that they had good feed; and it is no picnic to watch horses in heavy timber, for they break loose and wander off. Then he had to round them all up every morning, feed oats, and drive a four-horse rig all day. I must add that he kept his temper and stood the ordeal so well that his sweetheart married him soon after his return to Lander.

As we cross the borders of the Wonderland each step grows more enticing, and after the many years of waiting and the long, laborious journey, I demand much.

The shady avenues of young pines, lovely Moose Falls on Snake River, climbing the divide again into the Atlantic Basin, the live beaver homes and haunts, enchanting Lewis Falls and Lake and River, the noble forests of a thousand years' growth and the pure, rich color of mountain flowers— all is satisfying. How much greater the delight of descending into Yellowstone Valley!

The wonder and charm grew until, throwing care to the winds, yet with a firm grip on the pocketbook, we yielded to a delicious abandon, sure that every anticipation would be realized. Yet it is a pokerish kind of pleasure trying to enjoy the ravings of the demons from the bottomless pit at the "Thumb."

As for me I was kept busy counting the children. Every time one moved I felt certain he would stumble into a boiling, walloping vat of mud. That it was delicate rose, emerald, or heavenly blue mud did not reassure me. The children only laughed. Even the youngest pertly informed me he had not come all the way to Yellowstone Park to fall into a mud hole. Still the horrid smells and awful groans and the gaping mouths clear to Hades aroused such emotions of terror that in sheer desperation I hurried over to the lake. Playing with silver tipped waves or silver-tipped bears was safe in comparison.

The children know "Wahb" and "Johnny Bear" by heart, of course, so they eagerly followed the hotel guests along the little trail to the garbage glen to find if the Thompson Seton stories are true. They are all true. There was another little black Johnny Bear "who wanted to see." Another big lumbering Wahb, younger, maybe, but just as grizzly, and cinnamon bears and silver tips, growling and fighting over their food. I wasn't stampeded here as at the Thumb, for a stout fence separated us from the ferocious monsters.

Refreshed and in fine spirits we started early down the Hayden Valley, where we came in contact with the hard rules of the ark. One of them is that four-horse stagecoaches always have the right of way, and you have to turn out so as to give them the safe side. That is, if you are on a steep grade you have to turn out on the precipice side, giving them the inside, no matter whether you are turning to right or left and no matter if you have eight people and they but two. We were obliged to turn out that morning for ten separate coaches. Sometimes there are twenty coaches going along fifteen minutes apart.

But we didn't mind. We were too elated to mind. We had only sixteen miles to go and wanted time to enjoy every beautiful, exquisite prospect. Professor Nelson told us before starting not to fish in Yellowstone Lake or River because the fish are diseased. He said that scientists from the Smithsonian Institute had made careful study and gave it as their opinion that excretions from pelicans, which swarm on the lake, and which fish devour, contain a parasitic growth that infects the fish.

As we drove along the river's edge there were pools and shallows in which we saw hundreds of fish looking bruised and sickly, even showing naked bones, yet swimming about. Presently we passed riffles and cascades among which road workmen were fishing. They said fish that could live in a cataract were not diseased. Mr. Turnbull having only a secondhand account at best was not greatly impressed with the sick fish story, so he and our young driver were soon pulling out fine big rainbow trout. When they had a dozen we went on to lunch in a cozy meadow, dotted with lovely blue-fringed gentian close by the river's edge, though just beyond we noticed a steaming and a smelling.

The small boys hardly took time to eat, for they wanted to catch big fish, too. After lunch Mr. Turnbull proceeded to the beautiful trout. There was a coil of worms in the flesh or entrails of every fish. Then I fled for to tell the fisherman. They couldn't hear me call. I saw where their bare feet had gone around a patch of ground which appeared to be neither marsh nor sandbar—a crusty, shiny, disagreeable place. I could cut across. Not looking so much where I stepped but keeping the boys in sight, my feet burned. I knew then what it means to be over a lake of fire and brimstone. Good sprinting brought me to safety. Then we investigated the awful roaring from the cliff above.

On the side of a hill there was a great black chasm, partly filled with black mud that angrily flopped and spluttered and moaned. Around on the other side of the hill was a cavern. In it was a pool of boiling water that disappeared in the bowels of the hill, to reappear in a few moments, roaring and howling. There were other frightful mud geysers gaping like the jaws of Hades. I had walked on the crusted overflow. Again I fled fearing they would snap up my little people.

But the glory of Yellowstone Canyon speedily restored our nerves. Now are we most grandly repaid for every moment of weariness and anxiety of the journey, nearly six hundred miles long.

Tongue and pen and brush and camera are all inadequate to give a picture of the canyon, which for resplendent beauty in form and color stands unequaled, unique in the world. At Inspiration Point every soul was dumb with rapture. Even "Spring Jaws," as they call Tad, had nothing to say. He too, was enchanted, lifted to the seventh heaven, as it were, so that only twice, I think, did he squirm outside the rail over the precipice. To see him so impressed was great relief to all of us. Oh, it is wonderful to see a canyon so broad it is almost a valley, yet so deep you cannot hear a sound of the rushing torrent below; so brilliant in all the colors of the rainbow your eyes cannot bear it long; so studded with nature's architecture you see a thousand ruins of cathedrals and coliseums, and at the head of all a waterfall over three hundred feet in depth. Remember, Niagara is only one hundred sixty-five feet deep.

Of course, we remained here a day or two, sightseeing, cooking, resting, awaiting a telegram. It seemed sacrilegious to return to camp after that glorious gaze into nature's proudest wonderland and go baking beans, yet we had to have a change from Van Camp's. I wouldn't speak of it now only that is how we came to have a visit from a bear.

The beans were not done at bedtime, so I put in more wood, thinking they would be just right for breakfast. It was so hot the stove was outside. About midnight there was a great clatter of falling stove. Sure enough, a bear had tipped it over trying to get my beans. He was trying so hard to work the combination of the oven door that he never noticed our excitement. Not until I threw things at him would he go away. On the whole, I presume, we would have been disappointed if one bear, at least, had not paid us a visit. We never thought of being afraid, but I used all my ingenuity in hiding bacon and sugar from prowling bears, every night.

Captain Chittenden built a magnificent cement bridge over cascades, just above the falls. It was receiving finishing touches as we arrived on the scene. I thought at first it was a wooden bridge, but the wood was only a frame, for concrete masses of rock had been crushed in all sizes, in all dimensions. Immense floors for mixing cement were prepared and workmen came from every corner of the park—three hundred of them. Electric lights were strung, and for seventy consecutive hours cement and concrete poured into those wooden forms held by strong steel cables. The wood will remain all winter, and next summer there will appear a splendid bridge over which tourists may cross to the far side of Yellowstone Canyon, and by that means reach the foot of the Lower Falls. Those who have, through prodigious effort, arrived at the foot say that no idea of the height is apparent to standing at the brink. Of the three hundred ten feet, one third is lost in spray.

We spent the forenoon of the next day taking a last long look into the Grand Canyon of the Yellowstone. On our way back we found at the Canyon Hotel our expected message: "Will meet you at Mammoth Hot Springs, August 8th."

Oh then we flew as fast as our faithful horses could plod, for August 8th is tomorrow and Mammoth thirty miles away.

It is love that makes the world go round after all. Beauty may exalt, but love vitalizes. The mere thought of seeing our beloved so soon lent wings to our feet and new life to our hopes and joys, so that surmounting the divide which separates Yellowstone from Norris Basin was not so much work as a needed exercise for holding down our jubilation. The prospect of losing most of my responsibilities sent my spirits floating skyward.

We camped at Apollinaris Spring in a charming grove at the edge of a grassy glen. The very air seemed resonant with human life, and presently the children discovered a large party of Wylie tourists camping in the grove beyond.

They were very pleasant people, mostly schoolteachers from Fort Dodge, Iowa, and the vicinity, and we spent a happy evening getting acquainted.

We arrived in Mammoth five minutes ahead of the stage from the railway station at Gardiner. How we rushed to make camp homey. The driver quickly unhitched and had the horses grazing; Daughter, Tom, and Babe set the tent; Tad brought wood; Glad, water; and Mim speedily had a roaring fire; while I popped my biscuits in the oven, sliced bacon, seasoned corn, opened a jar of jam, and brought on the baked beans that were left, and set the coffee simmering.

Daughter watched the fire, Glad spread the tablecloth, Mim tidied the mess box, and the boys put the bedding to air in the hot sun. Then we had a moment to primp, wondering what Father would bring, for shoes and hats had seen hard service. Little Mim, sensing the hopelessness of primping said, "I wish he could bring me a new face."

But he never minded our weather-beaten appearance, though we had "roughed it" for five weeks. We all looked good to him, and the wonderful "springs" reflecting the joy of the occasion gleamed in rainbow tints.

Luncheon over, the strange formations soon attracted us. Pulpit Terrace, Jupiter Terrace, Liberty Cap, and Devil's Kitchen are intensely interesting—all are wonderful. These terraces are fully three hundred feet above the town but flowing toward the town. If I lived there I should be in constant fear that a fresh new boiling spring would spout in my cellar.

We have not seen all the wonders of the park—in fact, we are just halfway around; still we have reached the farthest limits and are six hundred miles from home.

Now a new spirit has entered camp. The businessman has come to take his family home. We have to hurry. Oats are increased threefold and threefold our speed. Then ho! For the geysers!

Now we must climb the hill from Mammoth, four miles long. But it is a fine smooth road of gentle, even grade and a magnificent view of snow-capped peaks, peaceful valleys, and age-old forests from Golden Gate. While the park roads are smooth as city streets, still you go up or down, up to mountain heights, and down to cool, dark canyons. As a matter of course there is no road in the world like it—a road 150 miles long that passes such variety of scenery—scenery so majestic, so wonderful, so beautiful, so horrible. And several times going over divides we saw altitudes marked on mile posts over 9,000 feet.

By and by we are back in Norris Basin, taking time to look at the Devil's Frying Pan and other steaming, sputtering curiosities. At the former spot was a guide board having several notes in pencil beneath the sign addressed to his Satanic Majesty. One read, "Dear Devil: We called on you today and were right glad to find you out, whooping it up for the other sinners. Now when it comes our turn, please dear Devil, we don't want to boil in your cave or bake in your kitchen or sizzle in your frying pan; give us the dynamite route—sudden and not too hot."

The Black Growler, a hideous, shrieking, hissing monster, we admire for his titanic and satanic power, but hastily pass on to cool, solid ground after a glance at the Hurricane, a mighty steam vent whose violent gusts are like the blast of a tempest. We camped in Gibbon Meadow that night and fished in Gibbon River. The next morning we drove slowly through Gibbon Canyon to admire the beauty of Gibbon Falls. Then we climbed another divide so as to get down into Firehole Basin, where the "hot times" really are, as the name indicates.

We lunched on the Firehole River fully ten miles below the Lower Geyser Basin, cool mountain brooks flowing into the river between, and yet the water was unnaturally warm.

We all went wading and were greatly fooled by the extraordinary clearness of the water. I'd guess it would come knee high, and find myself in up to the waist.

As we drew up on the bank of Firehole River today, there was a steep little pitch from the road to the ground above, just a deep rut. The horses could not pull evenly as one stood above it, the other below, so a whiffletree [part of a harness] snapped clear in two. That is to say, "the New Camp Spirit" took chances that the boy driver and I never did. But good luck was with us this day, too. In fifteen minutes a big freight outfit came along having an extra whiffletree that they very kindly loaned us.

I have inserted this good-luck story in here because I did not want to speak of the geysers, which come next, until I could have plenty of space for a full swing at them. You would naturally think when you had seen one geyser you had seen all. But there is as much variety in their form, action, and attractiveness as in the flowers and animals of the woods beyond. Some are natural fountains having bowls of rarest beauty; some build cones above a mound of rich lacework made of many-hued flint; some shoot straight, tall columns of water; some send up showers of dew drops. Some play independently and with the regularity of clockwork; some always wait for their elders to spout first.

Of the unnumbered thousands of steam vents, only the more important can be mentioned. It is nothing there to see a dozen tiny threads of steam puffing up in the middle of the road, while if we had just one in Laramie we would quickly build a summer resort around it.

The first geyser we saw in action was the Fountain, one of the finest in the Lower Basin. It is on a hill commanding a splendid view of the whole valley, and spouted a beautiful column of water ten or fifteen minutes. But its dear little neighbor, Clepsydra, which spouted immediately afterward, captured my heart. It sent up a sparkling shower of dew-drops no higher than a man's head that in the bright sun-shine resembled a lovely bush loaded with gems. One cannot understand the perfect transparency of the water until he realizes that every particle of animal, vegetable, mineral solids held in solution in cold springs is here completely boiled out, steamed out, and deposited long ago. To be sure there are pools so full of earthy substance that the steam only evaporates and wastes trying to purify itself—then we have the Paint Pots that have been mixing their paints a thousand years.

The most noted of these is the Mammoth Paint Pot just across the road from the Fountain Geyser. It is a pit fifty feet across, full of rich, smooth, strawberry ice cream, which somehow bubbles up six or eight feet, then drops back into exquisite roses and tulips. Quite a band of material has formed about the rim in a path soft and springy and smooth. The barefoot boys were cantering around it in great glee when I called them away, fearing one might stumble in, where he would disappear instantly, and forever. "Oh, Mamma!" said Tad, "I never had so much barefooted fun in my life!"

The Great Fountain Geyser is a mile beyond the Fountain. It is considered the chief wonder of the Lower Basin, but as I didn't see it play, we'll go on to Middle Basin, where there's something doing all the time.

Here is the famous "Hell's Half Acre," a vast seething cauldron 350 feet long and 200 feet across, twenty feet deep, with cliff-like edges on all sides but one. On that side, protected from winter's cold, and always having more than summer's heat, we found a yellow flower growing. It must have been a tropical plant, but how did it get there?

This huge boiling cauldron is now known to be a geyser and is named Excelsior. As a dynamic force it has no equal. Think of a body of water of such stupendous dimensions being hurled 200 feet in the air! Its last eruption occurred in 1888 when the volume of Firehole River was doubled. Captain Chittenden calls it a water volcano.

Five hundred feet west of Excelsior is Prismatic Lake, the largest, most beautiful spring in the whole region. Over the central bowl the water is a deep blue, changing to green toward the margin; while the shallow edges are yellow, shading into orange. Outside the rim is a brilliant red deposit, fading into browns, grays, purples. It rests on a self-built mound sloping gently in all directions.

Whenever the steam lifts so that the waters are visible, the play of colors is strikingly vivid. We were here when the sun was low so possibly the brilliant coloring was more dazzling than in midday.

Turquoise Spring nearby is a quiescent pool one hundred feet across, remarkable for its lovely transparent blue. When Excelsior played, the water in Turquoise sank ten feet and didn't recover its volume for a year. We made camp here just as quick as we could find a cool, safe spot, for we wanted the beauty of Prismatic Lake to sink deep, but unconsciously, the horror of "Hell's Half Acre" pressed deeper.

Up before sun the next morning such a weird, ghostly spectacle met us. Apparently, smoke stacks and steam engines are sending their cloudy columns above the dark foliage in all directions—yet no cities, no factories, only the silence of the forest.

A big day lies before us; we know we are approaching the climax of the park's wonders. Old Faithful, "The Guardian of the Valley," will appear around the next bend.

As we turn the corner and the Upper Basin spreads before us, we instinctively exclaim, "Dante's Inferno!" Here grouped, within a mile's space are the grandest, mightiest geysers in the world, and silent pools of scalding water, unequaled in beauty of form and delicacy of coloring. The entire valley is covered with a gray-white sepulchral deposit that is ghastly; clouds of vapor hang shroud-like above it; the earth trembles with a strange rumbling, the air is heavy with sulphur fumes and all vegetable life is extinct; though the forest presses like a dark fringe close around and emphasizes the ghastly look of death and destruction. To be sure the other basins were similar, but this is greater in degree, a culmination of it all, probably older than all.

The next thing to take the tourist's eye was the very appropriate nomenclature: Jewel Geyser, Biscuit Basin, Sapphire Pool, the Morning Glory, the Sponge, the Sawmill, Grotto, Castle, Giant, Punchbowl. Beyond all at the head of the valley on the summit of a self-made mound on a hill, stands Old Faithful. Captain Chittenden says, "Any other geyser, any five other geysers could be erased from the list better than part with Old Faithful." The Giant, Giantess, Grand, Splendid, Excelsior have more powerful eruptions. The Bee Hive is more artistic. Great Fountain has a more wonderful formation. But Old Faithful partakes in a high degree of all of these characteristics, and in addition has the invaluable quality of periodicity of action. It is in fact the most perfect of all known geysers. To it fell the honor of welcoming civilized man to this region. It was the first geyser named. In its eruption this geyser is very fascinating. Its graceful column rises with ease, to a height of 150 feet. The steam when carried laterally by a gentle breeze unfurls itself like an enormous flag from its watery standard.

With an average interval of sixty-five minutes, it varies little either way. Night and day, winter and summer, seen and unseen, this tremendous fountain has been playing for untold ages.

Only in thousands of years can its lifetime be reckoned; for the visible work it has wrought at its present infinitely slow rate of progress fairly appalls the inquirer who seeks to learn its real age.

Its daily work is enormous. The United States Geological Survey reports show the outpour for an average eruption to be not less than 1,500,000 gallons, which gives 33,225,300 gallons per day.

"The combination of conditions by which the supply of heat and water and the form of the tube are so perfectly adapted to their work, that even a chronometer is scarcely more regular in its action, is one of the miracles of nature."

We camped across the road from Old Faithful and saw it play five times; but we shouldn't have stopped there; we were taking chances. The park rules are very strict in regard to trespass on the formations, and thereby hangs a tale: But then, you would not expect such a large family to pass among a whole valley full of yawning gulfs and smiling springs and shooting geysers, absorbed until they forgot time and place and circumstance and not have something happen, would you? Since none of them fell into a hot spring, what could matter?

Well, "The New Camp Spirit" got arrested! And that mattered a good deal.

The horses found feed scarce in the very heavy timber so came into the open where the road lay. Just across, on forbidden territory, was a bunch of grass that poor Star wanted. Now he didn't intend to swallow Old Faithful, or tramp on its flinty surroundings. We were busy spreading a good, hot dinner on the tablecloth, so failed to notice Star quite quick enough. Presently we saw, and sent a boy to drive him back, but a soldier on horseback got ahead of him, and swearing like a trooper at boy and horse, he came thundering up saying, "Consider yourself under arrest, sir, and come with me!" In his very, very sweetest manner and most persuasive tone, Mr. Corthell asked, "May I finish my dinner first?" "Well, yes sir," the soldier said, somewhat mollified. And he sullenly stood in the background.

But dinner had lost its savor. This is an experience we had nowhere reckoned on. What if it meant jail—forgotten pocketbooks, broken wagons, floods, nothing ever created such consternation as this. But we didn't fall into a panic. The chief victim was so placid, so serene, even sweetly content, that the example set composed the rest of us. Before the walk to headquarters was over, sweetness won the day, so the fine was only two dollars when it might have been a hundred. From this point on the "New Camp Spirit" took no more chances and always put out his fires.

Again we cross the continental divide and are on the Pacific slope eight or ten miles, whence we have a magnificent view of Shoshone Lake and Teton Mountains. It is said there is another geyser system on Shoshone Lake, second only to that on Firehole River, but this is one of the side trips made on horseback which we cannot take. So ascending the divide again we drop down the Atlantic slope toward Yellowstone Valley. This time the Paint Pots at the Thumb really are beautiful and fascinating. Here is where you pull a fish out of the lake and throw it into a boiling spring, without taking a step.

As we are going home over the new Cody road, which begins at the wooden bridge over the Yellowstone River at its head, or where the lake pours into the river, why of course, we must detour to the canyon. I have quite a curiosity to know if Mud Volcano, Devil's Cave, etc., will appear so formidable to me as before. My husband thinks they are frightful—the most horrible sights he has met. I believe I put Hell's Half Acre first, in the list of my horrible; Black Growler second; and Mud Volcano third.

Like everybody else, we loved Old Faithful and the Morning Glory; we feared Excelsior; and we admired the Giant, Bee Hive, Punch Bowl, and a hundred other yawning chasms and smiling springs and spouting geysers. But the horrible rumbling as if an earthquake were imminent and the smell of brimstone made me eager to get my brood into the valley of safety beyond the Yellowstone.

We left the park for Laramie over a new road recently completed by Captain Chittenden, through Sylvan Pass and Shoshone Canyon to Cody. This is the crowning joy of the trip. The park swarmed with people. Wherever we pitched our tent, there hundreds had camped before us, to say nothing of the crowded hotels and Wylie tourists. But here in the heart of the mountain forest surely we are the first white woman and children to go over the trail, to fish in Sylvan Lake, to climb Grizzly Peak, to camp within the sacred haunts of Wahb, once lord of the Wind River Range.

Altogether we traveled twelve hundred miles, stood the journey well, and never, never had such a wonderful delightful summer. One must love the life to say that, must crave the outdoors and thrive on it. The sand was never too deep, the waters too high, or the way too long. Every obstruction made the goal a dearer prize, and we have lived our precious summer over and over.

Cold, thirst, hunger, fatigue, loneliness—I wanted the children to feel them all deeply, that their sympathy with the deprivation and isolation of the noble-hearted army who blaze the way for civilization may be keen, true, and sometimes helpful.

It is a trip anybody can take. It cost us only $25 apiece for the two months outing. We met people from Kansas and Salt Lake traveling just as we were. We had $15 worth of medicine along and never took a dose. The ammonia bottle was broken, also the camphor. The children emptied the witch hazel out in order to put specimens in. They plastered the arnica salve on the horses, and the dog ate the cold cream, and we shared our eight bottles of mosquito dope with ranchmen where we stopped. The wagon created some amusement on our arrival, for it bore the inscription, "July 4th, Park or Bust" on one side, and "September 1st, Park and Busted!" on the other. The children know their state as no book could teach them, and will have lifelong memories of the grandest scenes the world can produce.

STEPHEN M. DALE

—ɯɯ—

By the time Stephen Dale toured Yellowstone National Park in 1904, it had been transformed from a dangerous wilderness to a genteel resort. Railroads brought tourists from distant locations to the very edge of the park. The Army Corps of Engineers had built some of the best roads in America. And the Yellowstone Park Association had built luxury hotels that rivaled the best in the country. Most important for Dale, the park company had designed tours that sped travelers through Yellowstone in six days—less time than many early travelers spent at the Upper Geyser Basin.

Other than the fact that Dale wrote travel pieces, little is known about him. He probably toured the park as a guest of the park company, and he repaid their generosity with lavish praise. Also he gleefully repeated the stories told by guides who were notorious for spinning outlandish tales to glean tips. Dale's account of the stories he heard in the park conflates different explorations of the park and confuses toll road collector Yankee Jim George with Mountain Man Jim Bridger.

The following is a condensed version of Dale's trip, which first appeared in the Lady's Home Journal in August 1904.

THROUGH YELLOWSTONE
BY COACH—1904

From a story by Stephen M. Dale

"I didden wanta miss yer brekfusses, un the otha train leaves yeah fo' Gardiner in jes' an hour."

The hour was eight o'clock, and the voice was that of our friend of two days and nights' acquaintance, the loquacious porter of the sleeping car, which sometime through the night had been run on a siding at the Northern Pacific Railroad station, town, and junction, Livingston, Montana.

It was a beautiful morning and a beautiful place. It was August and the air was as fresh and crisp as in the East it would be in October. This very fact leaves all uninterrupted a wide view over an unbroken landscape to the tall bare mountains that surround the plain on every side. These mountains seem only a mile away but in reality are more than twenty miles; the clear air and rare atmosphere combine so to deceive the eye that they look near at hand and as clear-cut in outline as would some twenty-mile-distant object seen through a telescope.

But breakfast over, the conductor's cheery "All aboard," called from a train made up across the tracks, reminded us that our real destination, Yellowstone National Park, was some forty-five miles off, due south. At the end of this ride through the Gardiner Canyon, the train brought up, all of a sudden, at the very "Gateway of the Mountains." Even here

After the Yellowstone Park Company began using dozens of carriages to speed tourists through the park, the air became so dirty that passengers had to wear "dusters" to protect their clothing.
National Park Service photo

the engine stopped reluctantly, as though it also wanted to get through and roam about at will. While we climbed down, the train stood stamping and fuming at the wise regulation which has barred forever its entrance in though the archway over which there is inscribed: "For the benefit and enjoyment of the people."

No railroad or trolley line or other such route may either enter or cross the region, but there is a model wagon-road, built by the government, which extended from the main entrance through and back to it again, connecting the five important centers and as many different regions where things of most interest are found. At each of these points there has been constructed a good hotel, accommodating from a hundred and fifty to two hundred and fifty guests apiece, each one being a day's ride by stage from the one next before it on the route.

But there! I must be off, or I shall miss that stage. The company have got their baggage loaded on, have scrambled to the top, are talking all at once, and are shouting, each one trying to be heard above the other. If I shut my eyes, to this day I can see that driver gather up those six reins taut, I can hear him crack his twelve-foot whip and call out: "Down the line now, Boy! Come down the line!" I can see them come, six big Black Beauties on a gallop, round that curve, to the accompaniment of the most wonderful driving I have ever seen.

He who would get an idea of that 140-mile route over which we drove thus for six days must lay down clearly in his mind a figure of the letter Q inverted. The tail, four miles long, is the road leading from the entrance gateway to the first hotel, the one at the Terraces. Then let him stick four pins around the circle to locate the other four hotels in this order: the Fountain, the Upper Geyser Basin, the Lake, the Canyon; scratch three lunch stations on the three long drives of forty miles a day each; and he has it. Nor let him think that these drives are long or that the people get tired; the buoyancies of the climate and the exhilaration of such novel sights take care of that. Along this route there are a thousand spectacles, any one of which alone would gain a national reputation—and merit it—if it had chanced to be placed in some eastern state by itself.

And the most satisfactory feature of this six days' drive as a whole is the order of climax in which the sights along the way succeed each other. The six days of the journey are all differentiated, each by a special kind of spectacle, and each of these is a little greater than the one before. This happens because of two most fortunate, though wholly accidental circumstances: first, the more striking phenomena, although of five different kinds, are groups roughly, each kind in a district of its own—a district of only a couple of miles radius; and these districts, each one removed by just a day's drive from the one before; and second, the order of these groups' succession is in an order of progressive excellence. Each day presents not only a new but also a more engaging spectacle in beauty than the day before. When the journey is completed one imagines one's self having taken part in the rendition of some mighty overture—one strain after another being taken up and woven in and blended with the one or ones before, the volume swelling all the while until it reaches denouement in the roar of the Lower Falls and goes dying in reverberation down the canyon.

We entered the park that day at eleven o'clock and drove those four miles to the hotel at Mammoth Springs, reaching there for luncheon, and spent the first afternoon viewing the "Formation." No guide is needed: the strong smell of sulphur, the sight of steam rising from earth vents, and the brilliant coloring, all serve to locate the points of importance scattered over a three-mile circuit. The form the terraces take is due to the dripping of water over sharp ledges of regularly stratified rock cropping along the hillside. The most important of the terraces, their names suggesting their form and relative size, are the Angel, Pulpit, Minerva, and Jupiter. The last is the largest, covering several acres; the first is the most beautiful, being decked in every color of the rainbow.

After dinner there was a dance, as there is every evening in the hotel, with dress-suits, décolletage gowns, and a full orchestra rendering "Hiawatha" off here in the wilderness. But this will be the last appearance of such things. Tonight the baggage must be sorted and stored, as only one bag can be carried on the stage trip till we come back here.

At eight o'clock the next morning the party assembled on the hotel portico ready to start, the men all wisely wearing old clothes, expecting dust; the women dressed in dusters and blue goggles, looking like cocoons. We drove two miles through Silver Pass and Golden Gate past the Hoodoos and Bear Lake to Norris Basin. Here we stopped for luncheon for half an hour and begrudged even that short time—there was so much to see; then on to Emerald Pool and Obsidian Cliff. The road at this point was constructed in a novel manner. The use of blasting powder was out of the question, for the hill being of pure glass, no tools could be devised to drill holes in it. So fires were built along the edge and when it was expanded in this manner water was dashed on to break it into such fragments as could be removed.

At five o'clock we reached the Fountain Hotel at the centre of the second general region of interest. All about here are bubbling springs like a whole city full of factories has been buried underneath an avalanche with only their smokestacks and steam pipes reaching near the surface. The noise goes on underground like the sound of a Pittsburgh rolling mill, and the surface is all dotted with exhaust pits that remind one of great valves. What we heard was literally the far-off rumbling of that factory in which the very earth was made: for the forces at work here under our feet are the same forces that once tossed high these mountains yonder,

carved those slopes with the plowshare of glaciers, and furrowed these valleys with the blades of rivers. The feature
here is the Mammoth Paint Pot, a remarkable mud caldron,
fifty feet in diameter, in the basin of which is a mass of fluid
substance in a state of constant ebullition.

The drive the next day brought us by noon to the Upper
Geyser Basin, where we stayed noon and night. This is the
region of those things Indians called "Steamboat Springs,"
those strange eruptions of hot water that come from cones
raised above the surface of the ground and shaped like crater volcanoes. Normally these holes stand level full of boiling
water; they explode in tall straight columns from fifty feet in
height to two hundred and fifty, at irregular intervals varying from once an hour as in the case of that reliable friend of
the tourist, Old Faithful, to only once a week in the case of
the Giant, and lasting anywhere from the ten seconds of the
Economic to the ten hours of the Giantess.

It was twelve o'clock when the wagon brought up with a
swing at the camp here kept by one "Larry," a park character,
Irish by birth and also by brogue, who welcomes each guest
severally with a hearty handshake, serves fresh trout, hot
muffins, and gingerbread and Irish wit, and calls a geyser a
"geeser." "Hurry up now. Swallow yer lunch. For more luck's
wid ye than I know ye deserve. The Giant is due to play in
less than an hour." And so it did. So did three others through
the afternoon. We saw them all—saw sights so fearful also
that if Dante had known of them he might well have added
them, as other terrors, to his inferno.

The fourth day's trip was made only halfway by stage.
From Larry's to the Thumb Lunch Station—so named
because of its position on the thumb of land projecting out

into the lake—is twenty miles. From the thumb we crossed the lake by boat, twenty miles to the Lake Hotel, the stages following around the road to overtake us and be ready there to carry us again the next morning.

The lake is a beautiful body of water, but no one was thinking of that when we reached it: all were looking for what they had all heard of—the Hot Spring Cone. This hot spring boils so close to the cold water's edge that you can stand on the side of the cone, catch a fish in the cold water, and, without removing it from the hook, swing the line back over your head and cook it in the boiling water. And there are fish in the lake; so many, in fact, that a man who lets out boats and tackle here does so upon terms of a contract: "No fish; no pay"; so many that even the most bungling angler should not average less than one trout to half a dozen casts; so many that that evening after ten of us had come in from only two hours of this sport, the porter took the catch up to the hotel in a wheelbarrow; so many that—but there! That last one is a fairly good "fish story" even for the Yellowstone.

Before my credit is gone I must tell a "bear story" also. It illustrates the abundance of game in the park, and it shows how tame wild animals become where they may not be hunted. Every evening at all of the hotels, but more especially this one, because deepest in the forest, the bears come down to the back yard to feed on what has been thrown from the pantry after dinner. The bears learn to expect their dinner, and the people learn to expect the bears; and neither one is ever disappointed. That evening we counted twelve, and went close enough to them to take pictures of them.

The next day a short forenoon's drive brought us to the falls and the Grand Canyon. Here we stayed all day and night. Here is the climax, summit, zenith, every other word that means perfect fulfillment of one's hope—of all one ever hoped to see on this wonderful journey through the land of wonders. Here the word "falls" stands for a whole river's plunge over the edge of a precipice 365 feet, and the word "canyon" for a great rent in the earth six miles long, half a mile wide, fifteen hundred feet deep, where the earth seems to have fallen upon and disclosed a colored wardrobe and its chest of choicest jewels.

Here is a scene, which not even guidebooks can exaggerate: something that never has been perfectly described, nor ever will be. The only members of our party to attempt comment the next day were two. One was a lady who lamented: "Just to think! I chased away last summer over the ocean to look at that miserable little Tyrol when I might instead have come to Yellowstone." The other was "Dealy," our driver. Taking a hitch in his belt to brace him for descriptive narrative, he drawled: "I tell you, that there canyon is all right. Now, I've been driving stage for fourteen years, and I've heard people kick; but I never heard nobody kick about that canyon yet."

Besides these major features we passed many minor ones along the route, considered minor here only because of the size of the major ones with which they mingle: the Gibbon Falls, for instance. And the wildlife! One herd of a hundred elk in one band, a colony of beavers at work on a dam, mountain goats posed like statues on the summits of crags, and with fowl of every sort from ducks, many hundreds in a flock, to solitary eagles who put us to shame, when we thought we were at great altitudes, by soaring through the air a mile above us.

We did all the customary things, too, without doing which no journey would be thought complete; we got each one a souvenir, an old shoe or a hatchet coated with the hard formation where the water flows over the terraces; we cooked and ate an egg apiece boiled in the Punch Bowl; we drank from Apollinaris Spring; and listened to our names called back from Echo Canyon.

We heard the familiar stories told once at least to each party: heard of Yankee Jim variously known as James Bridger, the Pioneer of all Wonderland and the Daniel Boone of the Rocky Mountains; heard how he went back east in 1840 from exploring here, and told what he had seen and was regarded for his pains by being dubbed "The Monumental Liar of the North Pacific Slope"; or Colonel Hayden, the first government explorer here, and the sad tale of a member of that exploring party who got lost and wandered through the hills, till terrified by the uncanny sights he saw, and crazed by loneliness, he was found, after twenty-six days, creeping along the steep edge of a cliff on hands and knees gesticulating to the mountain goats and talking Latin to the eagles; hear of Electric Peak, which is so highly charged with loadstone that surveyors' instruments will not work there; heard of the Devil's Slide, his kitchen, his bathtub, and all the many other things named after him.

But any mere guidebook enumeration of its parts must fail to give any conception of the special charms of this place. This trip, distinct from every other, has a charm all its own. Nor is that charm a single one but rather manifold. First of all, there is the climate: it is only the water, or some of it, that is hot; the air is always cool—cool though never cold. Its invigorating freshness is due to the altitude—the average altitude of the park being higher than the top of Mount Washington. At midday it is warm and balmy as September, but in the morning one wears a light overcoat, and at night sleeps under blankets—and all of this in August. The evenings at the hotel are by no means the least enjoyable part of the day; there is that long summer twilight peculiar to the northern latitude, and all about are lovely paths bordered with shrubbery, which lead to porches filled with comfortable chairs, where one may breathe an atmosphere both restful and refreshing.

Nor am I quite sure that even yet I have quite touched the special charm of this trip. It is a place where one no longer thinks of tomorrow and still less of yesterday; a place where he loses all sense of time; a place where time passes so strangely and brings such confusion than one forgets the very day of the week. This last is literally true. On the third day out one member of the party of ten on our stage asked suddenly what day it was. All realized with the same surprise that it had not occurred to them to think for several days. Not one of the ten could tell either the day of the week or the date of the month, not even the driver, until he brought up from the depths of his coat pocket his meal ticket to see what date had been punched last.

And who were the people, these tourists, this party? In our party, of course, in every party, there were the usual types. There was the lady traveling alone, but such traveling is not unusual and is attended with neither danger nor inconvenience.

The whole party—in our case one of seventy-five people—traveled together all the way around for six days, keeping even the same seats on the same stages. Perhaps it is the view that intoxicates; perhaps it is the rare air; but whatever it is, people are more sociable and more natural here than they are elsewhere in all their lives in any other place.

No one as far as I can recall was ever introduced, nor was anyone told anybody's else name, but little things like that did not matter; names could be learned from hotel registers. Sometimes not even this trouble was taken; there was no time, there were too many interesting things to do. So nicknames were applied. There was "That Russian," "The German," "The Woman with the Bundle," "The Baby Elephant," and "The Heavenly Twins;" there were "Sunny Jim" and "Foxy Grandpa," "Everyman" and "That Other Man," while two young chaps who, because of their good nature and vivacity, because of the way they bandied one another and tossed back and forth good-natured raillery, were dubbed sometimes "The Baseball Battery," and sometimes "The End Man and the Interlocutor."

It was only when we got back to the starting point and there met strangers that we realized what old friends we had all become. On that last day of the tour parties break up with reluctance. In our party at least, friends of only six days' acquaintance separated sorrowing, and everyone exchanged cards with a neighbor. I have an idea, although it is a secret, that in the case of "The Yale Man," and "The Lady in the Newport Veil," "The Professor" and "That Girl with the Pretty Shirtwaist," "The Doctor" and "That Girl with the Gorgeous Eyes," other things may possibly have been exchanged. But then as "Dealy" says, "You can't sometimes most always tell."

It was dark that evening down the platform by the train and all the rest of us were busy with our baggage. What may have been exchanged since, nobody but the postman knows.

Suggested Reading

These books provide first-person accounts of nineteenth-century trips to Yellowstone National Park and should be readily available at libraries and bookstores.

Calvin Clawson, *A Ride to the Infernal Regions: Yellowstone's First Tourists* (edited by Eugene Lee Silliman). Helena, Montana: Riverbend, 2003.

The Earl of Dunraven, *The Great Divide: Travels in the Upper Yellowstone in the Summer of 1874* (introduction by Marshall Sprague). Lincoln: University of Nebraska Press, 1967.

Truman Everts, *Lost in the Yellowstone: Truman Everts's Thirty-Seven Days of Peril* (edited by Lee H. Whittlesey). Salt Lake City: University of Utah Press, 1995.

Nathaniel Pitt Langford, *The Discovery of Yellowstone Park* (foreword by Aubrey L. Haines). Lincoln: University of Nebraska Press, 1972.

Mary Bradshaw Richards, *Camping Out in the Yellowstone, 1882* (edited by William W. Slaughter). Salt Lake: University of Utah Press, 1994.

Osborne Russell, *Journal of a Trapper (1834–1843)* (edited by Aubrey L. Haines). Lincoln: University of Nebraska Press, 1965.

Richard Saunders, ed., *A Yellowstone Reader: The National Park in Popular Fiction, Folklore, and Verse.* Salt Lake City: University of Utah Press, 2003.

Paul Schullery, ed., *Old Yellowstone Days.* Boulder: Colorado Associated University Press, 1979; second edition in press, Albuquerque: University of New Mexico Press.

General W. E. Strong, *A Trip to the Yellowstone National Park in July, August, and September, 1875* (introduction by Richard A. Bartlett). Norman: University of Oklahoma Press, 1968.

Lee Whittlesey and Elizabeth Watry, eds., *Ho! For Wonderland: Travelers' Accounts of Yellowstone, 1872–1914.* Albuquerque: University of New Mexico Press, forthcoming, 2009.

George W. Wingate, *Through Yellowstone Park on Horseback* (introduction by Gordon B. Dodds). Moscow: University of Idaho Press, 1999.

Index

About the Author

M. Mark Miller is a fifth-generation Montanan who grew up on a ranch in southwest Montana 90 miles from Yellowstone National Park. His interest in early park travel began when he was a small boy listening to his grandmother's tales of baking bread in geysers and tossing red flannels into Old Faithful to tint the next eruption pink.

While attending the University of Montana, Miller worked as a reporter for the *Montana Standard* and the *Daily Missoulian*. After graduating, he worked for newspapers in Utah and Kentucky before earning a doctorate at Michigan

State University. He taught journalism for twenty-five years at the universities of Wisconsin and Tennessee.

Miller has been researching Yellowstone National Park since 2003. He has collected more than two hundred first-person accounts of park travel before 1915. His expertise on the history and literature of the park won him a position on the Speakers Bureau of Humanities Montana.

He is a judge for the Montana Book Award. His articles on Yellowstone Park and Montana history have appeared in the *Big Sky Journal* and the *Pioneer Museum Quarterly*. He is working on a novel for young adults about a fourteen-year-old boy's adventures in Yellowstone Park in 1871 and a history of Yellowstone travel for adults.

He lives with his wife in Bozeman, where he is a volunteer at the Pioneer Museum.